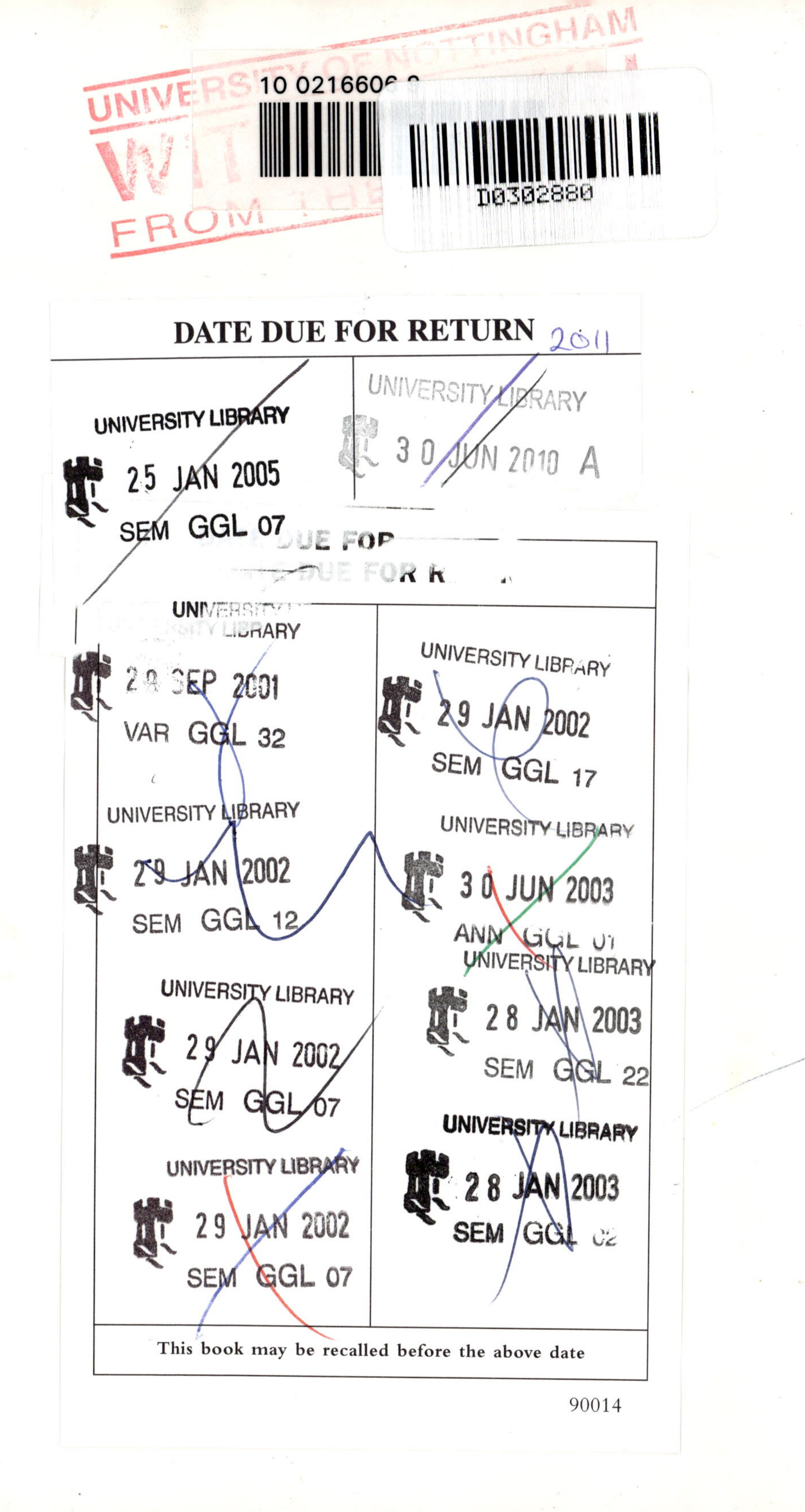

INDOOR AIR QUALITY ISSUES

INDOOR AIR QUALITY ISSUES

David L. Hansen, Ph.D.
Environmental Consultant

USA	Publishing Office	Taylor & Francis 29 West 35th Street New York, NY 10001-2299 Tel: (212)216-7800
	Distribution Center	Taylor & Francis 47 Runway Road, Suite G Levittown, PA 19057-4700 Tel: (215)269-0400 Fax: (215)269-0363
UK		Taylor & Francis 11 New Fetter Lane London EC4P 4EE Tel: 011 44 207 583 9855 Fax: 011 44 207 842 2298

INDOOR AIR QUALITY ISSUES

1 2 3 4 5 6 7 8 9 0

A CIP catalog record for this book is available from the British Library.

Library of Congress Cataloging-in-Publication Data

Hansen, David L.

Indoor air quality issues / David L. Hansen.

p. cm

Includes bibliographical references and index.

ISBN 1-56032-866-5 (alk. paper)

1. Indoor air pollution. 2. Air quality management. 3. Buildings—Environmental engineering. I. Title.

TD883.17 .H36 1999

363.739'2—dc21

99-35846

CIP

CONTENTS

INTRODUCTION

This book is a guide about the *nonindustrial indoor environment* and how it relates to the welfare and well-being of its occupants. It is designed for people in the environmental sciences/health field and will also appeal to readers interested in becoming environmental practitioners. However, since indoor environmental issues play such a large part in everyone's day-to-day existence, this book can also assist those who will not specialize in this field.

The book uses a multidisciplined approach in examining the causes and effects of the interactions between occupants and the nonindustrial environment (i.e., offices and homes). This multidisciplined approach encompasses numerous elements pertaining to the indoor environment, including medical aspects, chemical and microbial concerns, building design and ventilation systems, psychological aspects, conducting investigations, and pro-active programs to prevent problems.

It is essential to be aware that information in this field is increasing dramatically. In addition to whatever new books are published in the future, the primary sources for staying up to date are governmental agencies and professional organizations. The most important U.S. government agencies are the Environmental Protection Agency (EPA), the Centers for Disease Control (CDC), and the Occupational Safety and Health Administration (OSHA), which maintain websites and offer publications. Important professional organizations include the American Society of Heating, Refrigerating and Air-Conditioning Engineers (ASHRAE), the American Industrial Hygiene Association (AIHA), and the International Society of Indoor Air Quality and Climate (ISIAQ). In addition to their websites, these organizations publish journals, sponsor conferences, and issue conference proceedings.

LEARNING OUTCOMES

- An understanding of important facts and principles concerning the health and well-being of occupants in nonindustrial settings
- An understanding of how materials and conditions in nonindustrial settings can pose a threat to the health and welfare of the occupants
- An ability to apply principles to help mitigate problems and also to help prevent them

Text Structure

This book consists of eight chapters: (1) History and Evolution, (2) Building-associated Illnesses, (3) Building Design and Air Quality, (4) Volatile Organic Compounds, (5) Microbial Contamination, (6) Impact of Psychosocial and Other Factors, (7) Diagnosing IAQ Problems, (8) Pro-active Ways of Reducing IAQ Problems. Each chapter includes an overview, learning outcomes, discourse, suggestions for evaluation, key words and concepts, and two reference lists, one for the text and the other with suggested readings for additional information on the chapter topic.

Acknowledgments

I gratefully acknowledge the input of Drs. David Grimsrud and Richard Gammage. Their support and expertise were invaluable.

I wish to thank Dr. Claudia Sisson for her support and for the suggestion that led to this book.

Finally, I will be forever grateful to—and dedicate this book to—my wife, Ruth Charnes, whose love, understanding, and editorial talents have made this book possible.

Chapter 1

HISTORY AND EVOLUTION

OVERVIEW

The indoor environment is currently considered to be one of the most important health concerns for industrialized nations. How did this concern evolve? This chapter gives a brief overview of some of the major changes in the indoor environment and how those changes have impacted on occupants' comfort and health, concentrating on Europe and, most recently, the United States.

The chapter begins with a brief look at attempts to control the indoor temperature and at early theories about the impact of the indoor environment on occupants. The rest of the chapter reviews the significant changes in the indoor environment that began after World War II with a dramatic increase in the use of synthetic materials and chemicals that produced potentially harmful indoor contaminants. Next, the "energy crisis" of the early 1970s dramatically altered building design and ventilation to produce tight structures. The combination of synthetic materials and changes in building design are the major causes of poor indoor air quality today.

This chapter also looks at another crucial factor—peoples' perception of the indoor environment. Recent enormous media attention to potential health hazards like asbestos has promoted widespread fears that the indoor environment can cause cancer and other health problems.

LEARNING OUTCOMES

- A knowledge of the evolution of the indoor environment
- A greater understanding of the recent changes in the indoor environment
- An appreciation of the increased complexity of the indoor environment

EARLY DWELLINGS

Temperature and Comfort

The driving force throughout the evolution of the indoor environment has been comfort. Temperature is the parameter most closely associated with comfort, and a comfortable temperature has been the primary goal ever since people built permanent structures. Until relatively recently, most efforts concentrated on heating rather than cooling.

A comfortable temperature, generally considered about 72 degrees F, is essential for the perception of an acceptable indoor environment (Berglund 1989). Air that is significantly above a comfortable temperature will be perceived as stale and stuffy even if the air is actually fresh.

Hippocrates, in "Airs, Waters, and Places," states that climate has great effects on the physique, intelligence, and temper of people (Bedford 1964). Although Hippocrates was probably referring to the outdoor environment, the indoor "climate" controls comfort; which certainly impacts on an occupant's temperament and performance, if not intelligence and physique.

The Warming of Buildings

The earliest method of heating structures consisted of open fires, usually in the center of a room, with an opening such as a hole in the roof serving as a flue. The distribution of heat was uneven and considerable smoke was produced.

Wood, peat, and dung were among the earliest fuels used. Although coal was being used on a very limited basis by the end of the twelfth century, wood and charcoal were still the fuels of choice even in the seventeenth century (Bedford 1964).

Although emission studies were not done in centuries past, recent studies show that when emissions from indoor combustion (both smoke and gases) are not vented directly to the outdoors, significant levels of contaminants build up (Gammage 1984). How concentrated these contaminants are depends on many factors, including type of fuel and ventilation characteristics, but they can cause problems ranging from annoyance (eye irritation, for example) to severe pulmonary problems. Health problems from improperly vented combustion emissions still occur regularly in developing countries (Smith 1996).

One of the earliest techniques of warming a building without the problems associated with combustion products (smoke) was the Grecian hypocaust. In this system, hot gases from a fire accumulate in a sealed space under the floor and the whole floor essentially becomes a radiator.

The hypocaust was the first central heating system and it was no small accomplishment, because smoke and gases did not pour into the heated rooms. However, only the wealthy had this system; others made do with the more traditional "bonfire" with a hole in the roof to vent the smoke.

During the Roman Empire the hypocaust was refined to include hollow wall tiles; such systems were able to heat whole buildings without the problems associated with smoke and other by-products of combustion (Bedford 1964). With the fall of the Roman Empire, however, the hypocaust virtually disappeared.

The introduction of fireplaces, with chimneys allowing smoke to escape, provided a major improvement over open hearths. Chimneys were being used in Italy by the fourteenth century and in England by the fifteenth century (Bedford 1964). Again, chimneys were only for the wealthy, and as late as the seventeenth century the poor did not have chimneys in their homes.

The design of fireplaces kept improving to produce a more even room temperature and to remove smoke, which was still considered an annoyance rather than a health hazard. As coal became more popular, efforts to curtail smoky chimneys included the development of the open coal grate.

A breakthrough occurred in the early 1700s when Gauger designed a fireplace in which outside air could be heated and passed into the room (Bedford 1964). Gauger claimed that his fireplace was a "perfect specific against the annoyance of smoke in rooms, which smutched everything in the apartments, and particularly the lace, linen, skin and eyes of the ladies" (Bedford 1964).

Central Heating

Improvements in fireplace design provided more comfort for smaller residential spaces, but fireplaces were not adequate for heating larger spaces. Larger spaces began to be heated by enclosed systems such as stoves.

In the late 1700s, hot-air furnaces, a technique that is still common, were introduced. In 1791, Hoyle obtained a patent for a steam-heating system, which rapidly became very popular. By the early 1900s, steam or hot water systems were being used to warm larger buildings. This type of system, called "central heating," creates steam or hot water at a central source and circulates it, via pipes and/or radiators, to heat a structure.

The next advance in heating was a large-scale extension of central heating called "district heating," in which steam plants heat groups of buildings instead of just one structure. Such systems are now common. In large cities, a single supplier may heat a majority of the larger buildings.

These systems eliminated the need for fireplaces as well as the indoor pollution associated with them. However, early steam plants used coal—usually soft coal with high sulfur content—as a source of energy. They were a significant source of *pollution*, which in turn could be brought into a building by mechanical or natural ventilation.

Air Conditioning

One of the first successful efforts to cool the air was developed in the mid 1800s by a physician, Dr. John Gorrie. Initially, Gorrie tried blowing air over ice in an attempt to give his patients relief from the hot Florida climate. He then developed a mechanical refrigeration system using a compressor, which is still an essential component of air conditioners (Proctor 1982). Although the first commercial air conditioner was produced by Willis Carrier in 1914, cooling systems did not become common for many decades. Today, their widespread use permits year-round control of interior temperatures.

Ventilation

Initially, only natural ventilation was available; this relied on open windows and structure "leaks" created by doors and other building components. During the early eighteenth century, ventilation by mechanical means was introduced when Desagliers invented a hand-operated centrifugal fan that could bring fresh air into a building or extract air. This method was used in 1736 for ventilating the House of Commons (Bedford 1964).

The invention of electric fans permitted mechanical ventilation to became an important method for introducing and directing outside air throughout buildings. Mechanical ventilation is especially important in large buildings that are subdivided into small offices, since natural ventilation (such as opened windows) is not adequate in such situations.

Today, the introduction of conditioned fresh air into a building is controlled by complex heating, ventilating, and air conditioning (HVAC) systems. How HVAC systems impact on the indoor environment is discussed in the chapters on building design and microbial contamination.

THEORIES ABOUT AIRBORNE CONTAMINATION

In the past, there was little information about the relationship between smoke and health, and smoke was regarded merely as an annoyance. Most people, especially those without the resources to have a fireplace with a good flue, certainly were more concerned with warmth than with annoyances.

Moreover, the first concerns about the emissions from fires focused on the outdoor environment, not the indoor. In London, for example, as far back as the seventeenth century, outdoor air pollution was a major environmental concern. In 1661, John Evely wrote a treatise to King Charles II entitled "Fumigium, or the Inconvenience of the Aer and Smoak of London Dissipated." Evely observes, "The air is here eclipsed with such a cloud of sulphure, as the sun itself is hardly able to penetrate and the weary traveller at many miles distance sooner smells than sees the city to which he repairs" (Singh 1995).

In 1733, John Arbuthnot, physician to Queen Anne, published a book on the effects of air on human bodies. He too noted the impact of fuel emissions, writing, "The air of Cities is not so friendly to the lungs as that of the Country, for it is replete with Sulphorous Streams of Fuel" (Arbuthnot, 1733).

Those early scientists who looked at the indoor environment had various theories, some about comfort, others about health. For example, it was generally accepted that because crowded rooms were excessively warm, the discomfort experienced was attributable solely to the temperature. Gauger, whose fireplace improvements are discussed earlier in this chapter, disagreed. He believed that it was not the warmth of a room that caused problems, but its inequality of temperature and lack of ventilation (Gauger 1714).

In the late eighteenth century, Lavoisier studied the composition of air in occupied indoor environments, and his work "did not hesitate to attribute to carbonic acid the malaise generally attributed to warmth alone" (Leblanc 1842). For more than 100 years, people subscribed to Lavoisier's theory that an excess of carbon dioxide from respiration in overcrowded rooms caused the discomfort experienced (Bedford 1964).

Approximately 150 years ago, D. B. Reid recognized the importance of a good indoor environment. He wrote, "Mental anxiety may, perhaps, be considered the most powerful enemy to the duration of human life, and, next to it, defective nutriment, whether in quantity or quality. But after these, no other cause, at least in modern times, appears to have inflicted so great an amount of evil upon the human race as defective ventilation" (Reid 1848).

Reid, like Gauger before him, believed that ventilation was an essential component of the quality of an indoor environment. He was concerned with the amount of fresh air supplied to the indoor environment and also the chemical and physical properties of the air. Reid was remarkably perceptive about the influence of the indoor environment on our well-being.

In the mid 1850s, a major shift in Lavoisier's carbon dioxide theory was proposed by Pettenkofer, a professor of hygiene in Munich who lectured on health-related issues (Sundell 1994). Pettenkofer proposed that "the unpleasant symptoms were not due merely to warmth or humidity, or to carbon dioxide excess or oxygen deficiency, but rather to the presence of very small quantities of organic material from the skin and lungs" (Pettenkofer 1862). Pettenkofer felt that the concentration of carbon dioxide was an indicator of airborne contamination that could cause problems but not the culprit (Bedford 1964). Pettenkofer and a number of other authors of his time suggested 1000 ppm of carbon dioxide as a limit value for an adequately ventilated room (Sundell 1994). These theorists were right about the role of carbon dioxide as an indicator, and carbon dioxide concentrations are currently measured when monitoring ventilation. This is discussed in more detail in the chapter on building design.

During the late nineteenth century, researchers studying contaminants in indoor air looked for evidence of toxicity from expired breath. This concept, called the "anthropotoxin theory," could not be proved, and lack of ventilation continued to be associated with discomfort and not health (Bedford 1964). Although later researchers were able to show that occupants of poorly ventilated rooms experienced discomfort and loss of appetite, they were not able to show the cause of discomfort (Winslow 1915).

In the early part of this century, research by Hill demonstrated the importance of air movement as a comfort factor. In Hill's experiments, eight students were placed in a small (3 cubic meters) airtight chamber with provision for heating and cooling, and with electric fans for creating air movement. Hill found the students' thermal discomfort was relieved to an astonishing extent by putting on the fans, even if the temperature was not changed (Hill 1914). These experiments showed that the speed of air movement, as well as its temperature and humidity, exerts a profound effect on comfort. Hill reported that "although the purity of the air of occupied rooms is of no small importance, the prime consideration from the standpoint of comfort is that the physical environment shall be suitable" (Hill 1914).

In 1936, Yaglou published a landmark paper on ventilation requirements for the reduction of body odor (Yaglou 1936). Yaglou's research on threshold levels of body odor led to the American Standards Association standard of 10 cubic feet per minute (cfm) of fresh air per person. He also realized that temperature is one of the most significant factors in air quality, noting that "unless it is controlled the quality will suffer badly no matter what the outdoor air supply, particularly when the air is overheated." Today, temperature is considered one of the most important factors determining acceptable air quality.

MODERN ERA (POST–WORLD WAR II)

Problems associated with the contemporary indoor environment are not limited to the United States and can be found in many industrialized nations. However, this chapter limits discussions to the United States not only for practical reasons but also because (1) the United States experienced the great growth in post–World War II construction, (2) the United States was one of the first to recognize the importance of environmental health issues, and (3) the United States has various climatic conditions that create different indoor air quality (IAQ) situations.

Synthetic Construction Materials

The period following World War II was a time of great growth for the United States, with a tremendous amount of building, particularly for housing, manufacturing complexes, and office buildings. The supply of natural materials such as wood necessary to keep up with this insatiable demand diminished. A wide range of synthetic materials was introduced: buildings were constructed of pressed wood and fiberboard products and furniture and other furnishings were increasingly made of synthetic composites. These synthetic structural and decorative materials became one of the most significant sources of indoor pollution (see the chapter on chemical contamination).

At the same time, the use of various chemicals grew at an unimaginable pace. Chemical cleaners, office supplies, pesticides, etc., became ubiquitous, adding to indoor pollution.

Energy Crisis

A second factor that dramatically altered the indoor environment, particularly of office complexes, was the energy crisis of 1973–74, when the price of oil in the United States increased from $3 to $30 per barrel. This significantly influenced how buildings were designed and operated.

Buildings consume 60% of the electricity and 40% of the natural gas used in the United States (American Institute of Architects 1994). The predominant energy-related cost of running an office complex is the cost of ventilation—bringing fresh air into a building and heating, cooling, or moving the air with a fan system. During the energy crisis, the very first concern for building owners and managers was to reduce this cost. An immediate way to do so was to reduce outdoor air by (1) shutting outside dampers, (2) turning fans off completely, and (3) reducing fan speed. For example, even a 20% reduction in fan speed translates into a 50% reduction in fan power. The energy reduction is larger since less outdoor air needs to be conditioned. However, reducing outside air allows a greater potential for a buildup of contaminants.

An effective way of reducing cost for residential complexes was to "tighten the building," decreasing the amount of air exchanged through the infiltration of outside air. By reducing the leakage of the building envelope, the cost of controlling a building's temperature (either by cooling or heating) was substantially lowered. This was accomplished by numerous techniques: insulation was increased, vapor barriers were installed, and major leakage areas such as windows were sealed.

The inability to open windows would have severe consequences, not only because of the obvious physical implications but also because of the psychological impact on occupants. The impact on building ventilation systems was significant since mechanical ventilation systems were now necessary to bring in sufficient fresh air. The psychological impact on people was also extreme, since occupants could no longer control their environment by opening or closing windows.

As buildings became more complex, and awareness of the impact of the indoor environment on occupants increased, there was increasing need for guidelines about the indoor environment. The group most influential in developing guidelines that become building standards is the American Society of Heating, Refrigerating and Air Conditioning Engineers (ASHRAE), an international nonprofit organization founded in 1895. In 1975, the need to conserve energy prompted ASHRAE to reduce its recommendations for minimum ventilation rates from 15 cfm per person to 5 cfm per person. ASHRAE also published a standard on the design of energy efficient buildings—Standard 90-75, "Energy Conservation in New Building Design."

These ASHRAE standards had a significant impact on the indoor environment. An ASHRAE member recently stated, "As these issues [changes in ventilation and building design] came together, they led to the indoor air quality problems we have today" (Coad 1996).

HEALTH CONCERNS

In the early 1700s, the major environmental health concern was not indoor pollution but ambient outdoor pollution caused by smoke emissions from fireplaces. In the early 1970s, the focus was also on outdoor air, with emissions from automobiles and industrial smokestacks of primary concern (Singh 1995).

In the mid 1970s, indoor pollution began to receive increased public attention. The two major culprits that increased public awareness were a volatile organic compound—formaldehyde—and a naturally occurring mineral—asbestos.

Formaldehyde, one of the most widely produced chemicals, with annual production in excess of 5 billion pounds, is used in a variety of building products. However, to date the biggest health problems have been associated with pressed wood and with urea formaldehyde foam insulation (UFFI). These two building materials have produced the majority of severe health complaints by building occupants (Gammage 1984).

Since products containing formaldehyde were prevalent in so many building materials, media attention to the problems became a catalyst for enhancing public awareness about indoor environmental factors causing health problems.

Asbestos was even more instrumental in pushing the indoor environment into the limelight. Although asbestos had long been recognized as a health hazard in the industrial workplace, in the 1980s asbestos was also recognized as a potential health hazard in offices and schools. In 1983, the EPA made the provocative statement that "exposure to airborne asbestos, regardless of the level, involves some health risk" (EPA 1983).

Concern about any airborne level of asbestos, along with the long latency period involved in asbestos-related disease, caused enormous media attention. Fear of asbestos in indoor settings became one of the largest single environmental health concerns this nation has had to date, promoting fears that the indoor environment could cause cancer and other health problems. The public demanded the removal of asbestos in schools and an asbestos-free work environment.

In the late 1980s, new scientific information revealed that the health risks for building occupants exposed to asbestos were actually very low (Mossman 1990). But people do not simply disregard scientific information about risks. Instead, they consider this information in combination with their perceptions of the social, political, and ethical characteristics of the risk. This topic is discussed in more detail in the chapter on psychological issues.

Although the asbestos hysteria of the 1980s has abated somewhat, building occupants increasingly question their well-being in places that previously were considered safe, and the focus on the nonindustrial workplace has intensified. More recent findings concerning health are discussed in the chapter on medical aspects.

SUMMARY

The early use of open fires with fuels such as wood, charcoal, and coal to produce warmth probably was the first major source of indoor contaminants. Body odor, primarily an annoyance, was also a consideration in early indoor environments. The development of indirect central heating methods eliminated indoor smoke and dramatic temperature variations, although body odor remained a problem. The introduction of mechanical ventilation systems helped augment natural ventilation, bringing fresh air into a building and reducing the body odor problem.

The increased demand for construction materials after World War II led to the use of numerous synthetic materials, and contaminants from these products became a significant source of indoor contamination. In addition, the energy crisis of the early 1970s led to altered building design, with buildings' outer envelope sealed and ventilation reduced. These two factors caused the indoor environment to become a major health issue. At the same time, enormous media attention on the dangers of asbestos raised public awareness—and fears—about the indoor environment.

SUGGESTIONS FOR EVALUATION

- Give an overview of the major changes in the indoor environment.
- Define the events that impacted on the indoor environment after World War II.
- Discuss the role that formaldehyde and asbestos played in promoting concern about the indoor environment.

KEY WORDS AND CONCEPTS

Temperature, body odor, carbon dioxide, mechanical ventilation, smoke, energy conservation, central heating, district heating, tight building, asbestos, formaldehyde, synthetic building materials

REFERENCES

American Institute of Architects, *Environmental Resource Guide* (1994), AIA, Washington.

Arbuthnot, J., *An Essay Concerning the Effects of Air on Human Bodies* (1733), J. Tonson, London.

Bedford, T., *Basic Principles of Ventilation and Heating* (1964), H. K. Lewis and Co. Ltd., London.

Berglund, L., and Cain, W. S., "Perceived Air Quality and the Thermal Environment," *The Human Equation: Health and Comfort* (1989), ASHRAE, Atlanta.

Coad, W. J. (1996), "Indoor Air Quality: A Design Parameter" *ASHRAE J.*, Vol. 38, #6.

EPA, *Guidance for controlling asbestos-containing materials in buildings* (1983), Washington, DC: EPA 560/5-83-002.

Gauger, N., *La mechanique du feu* (1714), H. Schelte, Amsterdam.

Gammage, R., and Kaye S. (eds.), *Indoor Air and Human Health* (1984), Lewis Publishers, Inc., Chelsea, MI.

Hill, L. (1914), "Report on Ventilation and the Effect of Open Air and Wind on the Respiratory Metabolism," *Rep. Loc. Bd. Publ. Health, N. S.*

Leblanc, F. (1842), "Recherches sur la composition de l'air confine," *Ann. Chim. Phys.*, 5, 223.

Mencken, H. L., *A New Dictionary of Quotations* (1942), A. A. Knopf, New York.

Mossman, B., Bignon, J., Corn, M., Seaton, A., and Gee, J. (1990), "Asbestos: Scientific

Developments and Implications for Public Policy," *Science,* 247:294–300.

Pettenkofer, M. (1862), "Ueber die Respiration," *Ann. Chem. Pharm.*, Supplement 2.1.

Proctor, D., and Andersen, I. B. (eds.), *The Nose: Upper Airway Physiology and the Atmospheric Environment* (1982), Elsevier Biomedical Press, New York.

Reid, D., B., *Illustrations of the Theory and Practice of Ventilation* (1848), Longman, Brown, Green and Longsmans, London.

Singh, H. B., *Composition, Chemistry, and Climate of the Atmosphere* (1995), Van Nostrand Reinhold Books, New York.

Smith, K. R. (1996), "Indoor Air Pollution in Developing Counties: Growing Evidence of Its Role in the Global Disease Burden," *Indoor Air '96*, Vol. 3, Nagoya, Japan.

Sundell, J. (1994) "On the Association Between Building Ventilation Characteristics, Some Indoor Environmental Exposures, Some Allergic Manifestations and Subjective Symptom Reports," *Indoor Air*, Vol. 4; Supplement #2.

Winslow, C. E. A., and Palmer, G. T. (1915), "The effect upon appetite of the chemical constituents of the air of occupied rooms," Proc. Soc. Exp. Biol. Med., 12, 141.

Yaglou, C. P., Riley, E. C., and Coggins, D. I., (1936), "Ventilation requirements," ASHRAE, *Transaction,* 42, Atlanta.

SUGGESTED READINGS

ASHRAE, *Heat and Cold: Mastering the Great Indoors* (1996), ASHRAE, Atlanta.

Bedford, T., *Basic Principles of Ventilation and Heating* (1964), H. K. Lewis and Co. Ltd., London.

Gammage, R., and Kaye, S. (eds.), *Indoor Air and Human Health* (1984) Lewis Publishers, Inc., Chelsea, MI.

Mossman, B., Bignon, J., Corn, M., Seaton, A., and Gee, J. (1990), "Asbestos: Scientific Developments and Implications for Public Policy," *Science,* 247:294–300.

Sundell, J. (1994), "On the Association Between Building Ventilation Characteristics, Some Indoor Environmental Exposures, Some Allergic Manifestations and Subjective Symptom Reports," *Indoor Air*, Vol. 4; Supplement 2

Yaglou, C. P., Riley, E. C., and Coggins, D.I. (1936), "Ventilation Requirements" ASHRAE, *Transaction*, 42, Atlanta.

Chapter 2

BUILDING-ASSOCIATED ILLNESSES

OVERVIEW

The Occupational Safety and Health Administration (OSHA) has estimated that 30 to 70 million American workers are affected by nonoccupational building-related environmental problems (BNA 1992). Occupational diseases associated with the traditional *industrial* workplace are estimated to be 350,000 new cases each year (Landrigan 1991). This disparity in the numbers of workers affected by their work environment is attributable in part to the difference in health concerns in the two.

This chapter identifies some of the different adverse health effects observed in industrial and nonindustrial settings. The beginning of the chapter deals with occupational health and the difficulty of applying classical industrial hygiene standards and traditional occupational approaches to the nonindustrial environment. The latter part of the chapter focuses on building-associated illnesses in the nonindustrial environment.

It is important to note that there is currently a great deal of research on the indoor environment, especially on relevant health issues. The chapter provides an overview and deals with general concepts, with suggested references to supply more specific information, but readers are advised to keep current as new information becomes available.

LEARNING OUTCOMES

- A knowledge of the major health issues in the nonindustrial environment
- A greater understanding of the difference between the adverse health effects of the industrial and nonindustrial environments
- An appreciation of the complexity of the health issues and the major influences on the growing nonindustrial workforce

OCCUPATIONAL HEALTH IN THE INDUSTRIAL ENVIRONMENT

The industrial indoor environment has long been known to be associated with clinically evident adverse health effects. Causal associations have long been established between toxic occupational exposures and diseases of many organ systems (Landrigan 1991). Lead poisoning is the oldest recorded occupational disease; and Hippocrates, in the fourth century B.C., is credited with being the first to record adverse effects from exposure to lead by mine workers (Clayton 1978). Many others have looked at the relationship of health and occupations; as early as 1700, Rammazzini published a book on occupational diseases, discussing diseases resulting from dusts, metal fumes, and chemicals (Clayton 1978).

This focus on industrial workers increased over time. Because of concern for the health and safety of industrial workers, Public Law 91-596, commonly known as the Occupational Safety and Health Act (OSHA), was passed in 1970. It was designed to protect workers from unhealthy working conditions in industrial settings. One of the basic provisions of the act was to establish standards for health and safety and "to provide for the general welfare to assure so far as possible every man and woman in the nation safe and healthful working conditions." "Safe and healthful working conditions" was taken to mean the absence of associated diseases that a particular work environment was known to cause.

INDUSTRIAL EXPOSURE STANDARDS

Acting under the authority of the Occupational Safety and Health Act of 1970, the National Institute of Occupational Safety and Health (NIOSH), which is the technical arm of OSHA, develops and periodically revises recommended exposure limits for hazardous substances or conditions in the industrial workplace. These recommended exposure limits (RELs) are then published in the Federal Register and used in promulgating legal standards. Once the RELs become a legal standard, they are called permissible exposure levels (PELs) and are enforceable under law. These standards must be conformed to by industry and are the benchmark for deciding if an industrial workplace is "safe and healthy."

Another group that develops recommendations is the American Conference of Governmental Industrial Hygienists (ACGIH). This group was organized in 1938 to promote the awareness of occupational contaminate exposures and health effects (i.e., industrial hygiene). The ACGIH publishes guidelines for occupational exposures to airborne contaminants (ACGIH). These guidelines are referred to as threshold limit values (TLVs), and represent levels of contaminants that nearly all workers may be exposed to without adverse health effects.

Although only the PELs are enforceable by law through OSHA, both OSHA and ACGIH recommendations are based on the best available information from industrial experience, from experimental human and animal studies, and when possible, from a combination of the three. Generally, TLVs are lower than PELs because of the arduous process a PEL must undergo before it can become a standard. Thus, regulatory agencies have background information to be cognizant of the type of health problems associated with a particular industry. They can also suggest an acceptable contaminant concentration to which it is believed that nearly all workers may be repeatedly exposed without adverse health effects. As will be seen, the situation is not so clear cut in the nonindustrial workplace.

CURRENT RISK-ASSESSMENT PRACTICES FOR INDUSTRY

In 1983 the National Research Council released *Risk Assessment in the Federal Government: Managing the Process* (NRC 1983). This publication, known as the Red Book, defines most of the evaluation protocols used by the environmental-health risk-assessment community. The Red Book divides risk assessment into four steps: hazard identification, dose-response assessment, exposure assessment, and risk characterization. It states that "risk assessment entails the evaluation of information on the hazardous properties of substances, on the extent of human exposure to them, and on the characterization of the resulting risk." The risk assessments of the industrial workplace will change with new information concerning the hazard. However, most industries have well-defined exposure levels at which a contaminant can cause an increased risk of an identified adverse health effect.

Physicians can diagnosis industry-related illnesses based on a particular industry's history and etiology (i.e., cause of a disease as determined by medical diagnosis) of the illness involved. To help in characterizing health effects, ACGIH has taken the contaminants for which it has established standards and divided the various physiological effects into seven categories: (1) irritants—corrosive to mucous membranes, (2) asphyxiants—interference with tissue oxidation, (3) anesthetics and narcotics, (4) systemic poisons, (5) miscellaneous compounds, (6) human carcinogens and suspected carcinogens, and (7) reproductive problems (Breysse 1992).

In summary, the following general observations can be made about industrial settings:

- Causal associations have been established between toxic occupational exposure and disease.
- Physicians can identify work-related adverse health effects.
- Standards defining toxic exposures exist.

ADVERSE HEALTH EFFECTS IN THE NONINDUSTRIAL ENVIRONMENT

In contrast, the concept of health in the nonindustrial sector is defined as physical, mental, and social *well-being* rather than the absence of disease. Exposure standards that address these concerns do not exist. "Concepts of health have been variable across history, changing in response to societal expectations and understanding of the nature and causes of disease" (Sigerist 1943). Similarly, society constantly reevaluates its feelings about the indoor environment.

When the Federal Clean Air Act was passed in 1970, the air pollution–related health problems of greatest concern were thought to occur out-of-doors or in industrial settings. Since all buildings are immersed in outdoor air and since the major pollutant sources are outdoors, controlling these sources would automatically yield good outdoor air and good indoor air quality. Studies of indoor/outdoor concentration ratios showed that this was not an appropriate assumption. The focus was on illnesses such as respiratory disorders that were perceived to be caused by pollution generated by urbanization, industrial development, and the increasing use of motor vehicles (Singh 1996). The law did not even mention the quality of indoor air. Indoor air pollution was considered neither serious nor pervasive. In fact, the indoor environment was sometimes considered to be a place to protect oneself from outdoor pollutants such as automobile exhaust and emissions from industrial activities.

By the mid 1970s, indoor pollution began to receive increased public attention. In the late 1970s and early 1980s, formaldehyde off-gassing from pressed-wood products and urea-formaldehyde foam insulation produced the majority of severe health complaints by building occupants (Gammage 1984). However, the issue that was most instrumental in pushing the indoor environment into the limelight was asbestos. In the early 1980s, public attention focused on the health effects of asbestos in indoor settings, and extensive media coverage promoted fears that the indoor environment could cause cancer and other health problems.

It should be noted here that by the late 1980s new information revealed that the health risks for nonoccupational building exposures to asbestos were actually low (Mossman 1990). However, people do not simply disregard scientific information about risks. Instead, they consider this information in combination with their perceptions of the social, political, and ethical characteristics of the risk. These characteristics are called "outrage factors" (Hance 1988). The more outrage factors involved, the more likely people will be concerned, even if scientific data shows the risk to be small. This topic is discussed in more detail in the chapter on psychological issues.

As building occupants increasingly questioned their well-being in places that previously were considered safe, focus on the nonindustrial workplace has intensified.

BUILDING-ASSOCIATED ILLNESSES

Building-associated illness is generally considered the summary term for health problems in the nonindustrial environment such as office complexes (Cone 1989). Building-associated illnesses encompass (1) building-related illness, where there is illness with clinical abnormalities having a defined etiology, and (2) sick building syndrome, where there are complaints of adverse health effects but no clinical abnormalities and no defined etiology.

Building-Related Illness

Building-related illness (BRI) has been defined as a "clinical condition with defined symptoms and signs such as elevated temperature in which the attributable cause is building-related and identifiable" (Cone 1989). BRI is similar to industrial exposures in that the etiology is known and accepted. A diagnosis can be made by a physician on the basis of history and observations.

The most prevalent types of BRI are the hypersensitivity diseases, which include hypersensitivity pneumonitis, humidifier fever, building-related asthma, allergic rhinitis, and infections. These diseases are caused by exposure to antigens found in the building environment that stimulate a specific antibody response (Cone 1989). Most building-related antigens are assumed to be of fungal or bacterial origin and are more likely to effect people with a history of atopy (i.e., genetic predisposition to allergic manifestations). The resulting disease usually does not appear in large numbers of people, making a discovery of the cause/effect relationship between the building environment and the disease difficult for both patient and treating physician. The microbial source of the antigen is often not discovered, and in fact, may not be the patient's work environment. Unless the physician or patient is cognizant of the potential of BRI, the connection might never be made, and even if the building environment is suspected, there are no standards or guidelines that apply.

The following general statements can be made about BRI:

- A person who has any of the building-related illnesses has some type of clinical abnormality that does not go away when leaving the work environment and can be diagnosed by a physician.
- It will be difficult for the person who is ill or the treating physician to realize that the person's work environment is causing the problem unless something dramatic happened that directs them to the environment.
- BRI is usually a sporadic event.
- Microbial contamination of building components contribute significantly to BRI problems.

A good example of the difficulties of identifying the cause and effect of building-related illness is Legionnaires' disease. It is caused by *Legionella* bacteria and is by far one of the most notorious of the building-related infections since about 5 to 15% of known cases have been fatal (CDC 1999). The disease was first identified in 1976, when an outbreak caused severe illness and death among people who attended an American Legion convention in Philadelphia.

Legionella bacteria occur naturally in surface waters, including lakes, streams, and mud, but cooling towers, humidifiers, shower heads, and pipes containing warm water provide ideal conditions for growth of the bacteria. However, the mere presence of *Legionella* bacteria will not cause disease; the *Legionella*-contaminated water must be aerosolized and transported to people before the disease can occur, and building HVAC systems provide this transportation.

The Centers for Disease Control (CDC) estimates that 10,000 to 15,000 persons get Legionnaires' disease each year (CDC 1999). Outbreaks of Legionnaires' disease receive the most media attention, but most often the disease occurs as single, isolated cases not associated with any recognized outbreak. It is also estimated that between 1 and 27% of community-acquired pneumonias are due to Legionnaires' disease (Finegold 1988).

If pneumonia is diagnosed, most physicians would not test to determine if the disease is specifically Legionnaires' disease, nor would most hospitals routinely conduct such a test. Therefore the confirmation of Legionnaires' disease requires a special test not routinely performed on persons with pneumonia. To further complicate matters, the treatment for both Legionnaires' disease and pneumonia can be erythromycin. In essence, a physician may successfully treat the symptoms without making an accurate diagnosis.

In addition, a physician might not make any connection between the illness and the patient's work environment, and there is no formal mechanism in place to cover that possibility. If five people from the same building have Legionnaires' disease (which would be considered an outbreak), and each visits a different physician who successfully treats them with erythromycin but doesn't check for Legionnaires' disease, no one would suspect an outbreak or investigate if it was building-related. The CDC reports that "studies on antibody levels in healthy people such as blood donors indicate a relatively high level of exposure. This suggests that these organisms may play a larger role in human disease than has been suggested to date" (CDC 1999).

Sick Building Syndrome

Sick building syndrome (SBS) describes a situation in which reported symptoms among a population of building occupants can be associated with their presence in that building. Unlike BRI, where a person has an illness that can be diagnosed and clinically defined, SBS is associated with discomfort with the etiology unclear.

There are various definitions of the term SBS. The World Health Organization in the mid 1980s defined SBS as an increase in the frequency of building-occupant reported complaints associated with acute nonspecific symptoms in nonindustrial environments that improve while the occupants are away from the buildings. These nonspecific symptoms usually involve symptoms of the central nervous system (headache, fatigue, difficulty concentrating), irritation and a feeling of dryness of the mucous membranes, and skin problems (Sundell 1994).

NATO recommends the following definition: "Sick Building Syndrome (SBS) denotes a situation where a significant number of the occupants of a building complain of a typical group of general, unspecific, and irritative symptoms, including headache, dry eyes, blocked nose, and sore throat. The symptoms usually fade after the person has left the indoor environment but the specific cause is unidentified" (Maroni 1995).

Criteria for relating this syndrome to various indoor environmental risk factors has been developed, but not to particular causal exposures (Mendell 1996). Most of the time a diagnosis is made by eliminating all building-related illnesses, exemplified by no physical abnormalities when the person is given a medical examination. However, most people do not get a medical exam because of eye irritation or a headache that disappears after leaving their office. Workers may or may not consider their symptoms to be building-related.

A review and summary of the epidemiologic literature by Mendell in 1993 found that the following factors are most consistently associated with increased symptoms—air conditioning, carpets, more workers in a space, VDT use, low ventilation rates, job stress/dissatisfaction, allergies, asthma, and female gender. Each factor is quite complex and its role in producing or initiating an occupant's discomfort may not be straightforward.

For example, let's look in more detail at one of these factors—"more workers in a space." Certainly more workers in an area will effect the amount of fresh air per person, but what about other factors that are not as obvious: more paper usage, making the area dustier and perhaps causing allergic reactions; partitions separating the workers may change the air movement patterns; the fleecy material on partitions can serve as a sink for "contaminants" that will cause potential odor and irritancy; there may be renovations that involve the use of new materials and wet coatings that produce contaminants; more activities such as photocopying machines and VDTs; enhanced transmission of disease from person to person; or increased stress because some workers were moved to a new space they do not like. Each factor will be discussed in this book in the appropriate chapter.

Classical toxicology is inadequate to deal with issues of human discomfort (Ashford 1997). It is presumed that there is an interaction involving a number of environmental factors and sensory systems and that a number of personal, psychosocial, and work-related factors are associated with an increased risk of SBS (Berglund 1986).

Research is making progress in increasing our understanding of noncarcinogenic effects ranging from odor and irritation to chemical sensitization of susceptible individuals. Of particular importance is that building occupants are being exposed to low levels of complex mixtures of volatile organic compounds (VOCs). VOCs are emitted from a myriad of products through normal aging or during activities such as renovation or use of cleaning agents. However, the levels of VOCs found in nonindustrial settings are usually so low that they defy interpretation with industrial standards and corresponding health effects. But as discussed earlier, the adverse health effects for the industrial workplace with domination by single entities are not the same as for the office environment with a multiplicity of contaminants at low levels.

Some researchers believe that VOCs, even at very low levels, may play a significant role in building-related environmental complaints such as odor and irritation (Cometto-Muniz 1994). Others argue this is not a reasonable hypothesis since there is no clear medical model and insufficient knowledge to predict human sensory response.

Sensitivity and what role it plays in his/her response to low levels of contaminants may be key to some explanations of the cause of SBS and is also quite controversial. One definition of sensitivity is "those individuals who require relatively lower doses to induce a particular response are said to be more sensitive than those who would require relatively higher doses before experiencing the same responses" (Hattis 1987).

The factors that predispose people to be "sensitive" include age, sex, and genetic makeup; lifestyle and behavior, including nutritional and dietary factors; alcohol, tobacco, and drug use; environmental factors; and preexisting disease (Ashford 1997). To separate the issue of sensitivity from the purely environmental circumstances is an arduous task, perhaps an impossible one.

Very few topics concerning sensitivity issues are more provocative and produce such strong diversity of beliefs than multiple chemical sensitivity (MCS). People either subscribe to the concept that MCS is a clinical phenomenon or say it is simply "all in the mind." Although there is no universally accepted definition of MCS, Cullen offers the following definition: "Multiple chemical sensitivity is an acquired disorder characterized by recurrent symptoms, referable to multiple organ systems, occurring in response to demonstrable exposure to many chemically unrelated compounds at doses far below those established in the general population to cause harmful effects. No single widely accepted test of physiologic function can be shown to correlate with symptoms" (Cullen 1987).

Patients with full-blown MCS may exhibit a unique type of sensitivity in that the original sensitization be by one or a number of environmental agents (e.g., pesticides), but the subsequent triggering can be initiated by dissimilar chemicals at much lower exposures than initially encountered (Ashford 1997). Although MCS patients are a subset of the general population, more documentation of health effects may provide information that could play a significant role in solutions for building-associated illnesses for the general public.

FURTHER READING

This chapter provides a basic overview of building-associated illnesses and the suggested readings at the end of the chapter will add substantially to the reader's general knowledge. In addition, there are numerous specific topics that the reader should be aware of. A detailed examination of these issues is beyond the scope of this book, but some of the more major ones are as follows and can be found in the references: asbestos, multiple chemical sensitivity (MCS), radon, environmental tobacco smoke, and electromagnetic fields. On these and other topics, it is important to stay current because the indoor environmental field is evolving at a rapid pace.

SUMMARY

The traditional medical model used for industrial settings does not fit the nonindustrial workplace. In industrial settings, causal associations have been established between toxic occupational exposures and clinically evident adverse health effects with a focus only on life-threatening concerns. Standards have been established to provide a safe and healthful working environment. The concerns in the nonindustrial workplace are dramatically different: there is no specific occupational toxin to be monitored and the focus is on comfort and well-being issues.

In addition, there is a lack of knowledge of how the different physical and psychological stressors interact to produce the discomfort in nonindustrial settings. Etiology can be difficult to establish because many signs and symptoms are nonspecific, making diagnosis a distinct challenge. In sum, building-related health issues in nonindustrial settings pose many challenges to the health professional.

SUGGESTIONS FOR EVALUATION

- Define building-associated illnesses.
- Define the differences between the health issues in the industrial versus nonindustrial workplace.
- Give an overview of the health standards that exist and how they apply to both industrial and nonindustrial workplaces.
- What causes BRI and SBS? What are the difficulties a physician faces when evaluating a patient?
- What part does the occupant play in building-associated illnesses?

KEY CONCEPTS AND WORDS

OSHA, NIOSH, building-associated illness, building-related illness, permissible exposure levels, sick building syndrome, hypersensitivity diseases, chemical sensitivity, multiple chemical sensitivity

REFERENCES

ACGIH, "Threshold Limit Values and Biological Exposure Indices" (1995), American Conference of Governmental Industrial Hygienists, Cincinnati.

Ashford, N., and Miller, C., Chemical Exposures: Low Levels and High Stakes (1997), Van Nostrand Reinhold Books, New York.

Berglund, B., and Lindvall, T. (1986), "Sensory reactions to sick buildings," *Environment International,* 12:147–159.

BNA (1992), "Occupational Safety and Health Report," 921097.

Breysse, P. (1992), "The Development of Threshold Limit Values (TLVs)—Are They Appropriate for Use in Indoor Air Office Problems?" *IAQ '92—Environment for People,* ASHRAE, Atlanta.

Broome, C., and Fraser, D. (1979), "Epidemiologic Aspects of Legionellosis," *Epidemiol. Rev.,* 1:1–16.

Centers For Disease Control (1999), "Legionellosis: Legionnaires' Disease and Pontiac Fever," Division of Bacterial and Mycotic Diseases, Atlanta.

Centers For Disease Control "Morbidity and Mortality Weekly Report," published by CDC, Atlanta.

Clayton, G., and Clayton, F. (eds.), *Patty's Industrial Hygiene and Toxicology* (1978), third edition, Vol. 1, Wiley-Interscience, New York.

Cometto-Muniz, J., and Cain, W. (1994), "Perception of Odor and Nasal Pungency from Homologous Series of Volatile Organic Compounds," *Indoor Air,* 4:140–146.

Cone, J., and Hodgson, M. (eds.), *Problem Buildings: Building-associated Illness and the Sick Building Syndrome, Occupational Medicine: State of the Art Reviews* (1989), Hanley and Belfus, Philadelphia, 4 (4).

Cullen, M., "The Worker with Multiple Chemical Sensitivities: An Overview." In: Cullen, M. (ed.), *Workers with Multiple Chemical Sensitivities, Occupational Medicine: State of the Art Reviews* (1987a), Hanley and Belfus, Philadelphia, 2(4):801–804.

Finegold, S. (1988), "Legionnaires' Disease—still with us," *N. Engl. J. Med.,* 318:571–573.

Gammage, R., and Kaye S. (eds.), *Indoor Air and Human Health* (1984), Lewis Publishers, Inc., Chelsea, MI.

Hance, B., Chess, C., and Sandman, P. (1988), "Improving Dialogue with Communities: A Risk Communication Manual for Government," Department of Environmental Protection, Trenton, New Jersey.

Hattis, D. (1987), "Human Variability in Susceptibility to Toxic Chemicals: A Preliminary Analysis of Pharmacokinetics Data from Normal Volunteers," *Risk Analysis,* 7:415–426.

Landrigan, P., and Baker, D. (1991), "The Recognition and Control of Occupational Disease," *JAMA* 266 (5):676–680.

Maroni, M., Axelrad, R., and Bacaloni, A. (1995), "NATO's Efforts To Set Indoor Air Quality Guidelines And Standards," *American Industrial Hygiene Association Journal,* 56 (5).

Mendell, M. (1993), "Non-specific symptoms in office workers: a review and summary of the epidemiologic literature," *Indoor Air,* Vol. 3.

Mendell, M. J., Sieber, W. K., Dong, M. X., Malkin, R., and Wilcox, T. "Symptom Prevalence Distributions In U.S. Office Buildings Investigated By NIOSH For Indoor Environmental Quality Complaints" (1996). Presented at the Seventh International Conference on IAQ and Climate, Nagoya, Japan.

Mossman, B., Bignon, J., Corn, M., Seaton, A., and Gee, J. (1990), "Asbestos: Scientific Developments and Implications for Public Policy," *Science,* 247:294–300.

National Research Council (NRC), *Risk Assessment in the Federal Government: Managing the Process* (1983), National Academy Press, Washington.

Sigerist H., *Civilization and Disease* (1943), University of Chicago Press, Chicago.

Singh H. B. (ed.), *Composition, Chemistry, And Climate Of The Atmosphere* (1996), Van Nostrand Reinhold Books, New York.

Sundell, J. (1994), "On the Association Between Building Ventilation Characteristics, Some Indoor Environmental Exposures, Some Allergic Manifestations and Subjective Symptom Reports," *Indoor Air,* Suppplement 2.

SUGGESTED READINGS

Ashford, N., and Miller, C., *Chemical Exposures: Low Levels and High Stakes* (1997), Van Nostrand Reinhold Books, New York.

Cone, J., and Hodgson, M. (eds.), *Problem Buildings: Building-associated Illness and the Sick Building Syndrome, Occupational Medicine: State of the Art Reviews* (1989), Hanley and Belfus, Philadelphia, 4(4).

Clayton, G., and Clayton F. (eds.), *Patty's Industrial Hygiene and Toxicology* (1978), third revised edition, Vol. 1, Wiley-Interscience, New York.

Gammage R., Berven, B. (eds.), *Indoor Air and Human Health* (1996), Lewis Publishers, Boca Raton.

Godish, T., Sick Buildings (1997), CRC Press, Boca Raton.

Indoor Air '90, Fifth International Conference on Indoor Air Quality and Climate, Toronto, Ontario (1990).

Indoor Air '93, Sixth International Conference on Indoor Air Quality and Climate, Helsinki, Finland (1993).

"Indoor Air," Official Journal of the International Society of Indoor Air Quality and Climate, Munksgaard International Publishers, Copenhagen.

Weekes, D., and Gammage, R. (eds.), *The Practitioner's Approach to Indoor Air Quality Investigations: Proceedings of the Indoor Air Quality International Symposium* (1989), AIHA Publications, Washington.

Chapter 3

BUILDING DESIGN AND AIR QUALITY

OVERVIEW

This chapter is a brief overview of building design characteristics and their influence on indoor air quality. The chapter discusses the following topics: (1) site pollution characteristics, (2) general building design, and (3) ventilation and climate control. Interior construction materials and furnishings are mentioned but are discussed in detail in the chapters on volatile organics and pro-active techniques.

Although many building-related factors contribute to acceptable indoor air quality, heating, ventilation, and air conditioning (HVAC) systems play a dominate role in the indoor environment. Therefore, this chapter concentrates on such systems.

LEARNING OUTCOMES

- A knowledge of major building design concerns and their influence on air quality
- A basic understanding of HVAC systems
- An appreciation of the complexity of air distribution systems

SITE POLLUTION CHARACTERISTICS

Ambient Air Pollution

The quality of the ambient (i.e., outdoor) air is a crucial factor in maintaining a good indoor environment. Ambient air is pulled into a building by mechanical ventilation and used to dilute the pollutants produced inside the building. It can also infiltrate a building through uncontrolled openings such as doors, windows, and cracks.

The quality of ambient air is dependent on site location, surrounding population, and meteorological conditions. For example, ambient air in Los Angeles, known for its photochemical smog, is different from the less polluted air in cities such as Minneapolis.

Polluted air contains chemical vapors, gases, and particles that can harm people, animals, plants, and materials. Pollution sources are diverse and include motor vehicles and many types of industrial operations. The emission sources may be located close to a building or at a distance. In fact, pollutants can be generated in another state or country, with the contaminants being transported by air currents to a site hours or days later. In some cases (photochemical smog or acid rain, for example), the chemical precursors that form pollutants may originate miles away, and the conversion to more harmful pollutants occurs during transport (Singh 1996).

The EPA's "National Primary Ambient-Air Quality Standards" provides guidelines to evaluate the ambient air (EPA 1994). The EPA also regularly conducts air quality monitoring at various sites throughout the United States. The results are available, but it must be remembered that levels can change dramatically and suddenly due to meteorological conditions such as prolonged inversions.

If the ambient air is deemed unacceptable, there are few treatment options available. It is financially impractical to install air cleaners to reduce the level of gaseous pollutants brought into a building, and for the most part this is simply not done. However, by filtering the outside air, a substantial amount of particulate matter can be removed.

Usually, air pollution from general sources (sources in the community but not in close proximity to a site) is not a significant problem. There are, however, areas such as Los Angeles where topography, meteorological conditions, and emissions from motor vehicles contribute to severe ambient pollution problems. Even so, the regulations for reducing ambient air pollution levels are limited and pertain to reducing emissions from lawn mowers and the like; there are presently few regulations about cleaning the air being introduced into a building, because of the impractability of implementing such procedures. (However, strictly speaking, the intent of ASHRAE Standard 62-89 is to clean the ambient air if necessary before it enters the building.)

Local Sources of Pollution

Sources of pollution in close proximity or adjacent to a building can have a more dramatic effect than community-generated pollution. Local sources of contamination include drift from cooling towers, industrial operations, restaurant odors, and auto emissions from parking areas or highways; these sources can produce more elevated levels of contaminants than general ambient sources.

Often a temporary activity or disturbance causes high levels of contaminants. Construction, road paving, pesticide applications, wet-coating applications (painting, etc.), and other activities of even short duration can cause severe odor and irritation as well as anxiety. Odors in particular often present a vexing problem; their characteristics vary with changing mixtures and concentrations, making it difficult to trace their origin and to determine if the chemical or chemicals causing the odor are harmful. This issue can produce great anxiety, which is discussed in the chapter on psychological factors.

This type of problem—of short duration with high levels of pollutants—can be a major cause of unacceptable indoor air quality. However, unless the building openings or outdoor air intakes can be altered or closed if the high pollution pulse has a short duration (rarely the situation), the only option is to try to modify or reduce the source of pollution.

ASHRAE gives guidance on locating outdoor air intakes with respect to fixed pollution sources such as cooling towers in its document ASHRAE 62-89, "Ventilation for Acceptable Indoor Air Quality."

OVERALL BUILDING DESIGN

Commercial building design includes decisions about building shape and size, floor plans, location of pollution-generating activities, selection of materials, and general air distribution (HVAC systems). Indoor air quality concerns should include primary uses of the building, activities, or processes that generate contaminants, the presence of "special interest" groups such as day care centers, and any time-related demands on the ventilation system.

For environmental purposes, the building envelope should be constructed to control (1) water and water vapor penetration and (2) air infiltration (ASHRAE 1996). Reducing unwanted moisture in a building is very important for limiting problems associated with microbial growth, which is discussed in the chapters on microbial contamination and pro-active techniques. Uncontrolled air infiltration—introducing air not filtered for particulate removal— can interfere with the operation and maintenance of the ventilation system and directly influences the comfort and health of the building occupants.

Intrusion of unfiltered outside air into a building can be increased dramatically by natural forces. For example, a stack effect occurs as warm inside air rises in a building and the pressure differential sucks in cooler air on the lower levels of the building. Also, the wind can cause pressure differentials between the windward side of a building and the interior, inducing unfiltered air to enter a building.

One way to prevent the infiltration of unconditioned outdoor air is to have the building envelope under positive pressure relative to the outside air. This is achieved by bringing more air into a building than is exhausted; the result is a slight positive pressure indoors, which retards the infiltration of unwanted air. This technique reduces infiltration except through a controlled HVAC system, which filters the outside air before distributing it throughout the building. However, in terms of energy use this is an expensive fix.

Building Changes

As noted previously, sometimes a building's immediate surroundings change. In addition, a building's occupational patterns and activities may also change through renovations, new operations and/or equipment, different office layouts, etc.

So even if a building was originally designed to provide an acceptable air quality, changes in surroundings or internal activities can result in unacceptable conditions. Designing sufficient HVAC flexibility to address future IAQ concerns should be examined; however, experience shows it is not often implemented because of the cost.

VENTILATION AND CLIMATE CONTROL

In most nonresidential buildings, even those with operable windows, ventilation is accomplished by mechanical means. Mechanical ventilation systems are designed to bring in outside air, heat or cool it, and distribute this air throughout the building and remove stale air. A typical system consists of controls to regulate the amount and temperature of ventilation air; fans to move the air; filters to clean the air; coils for heating and/or cooling the air; dampers for regulating the flow of air; and a distribution system that brings ventilation air to occupants and vents air from occupied space to mix with outside air (Bearg 1993).

This type of mechanical ventilation system is called an HVAC (heating, ventilation, and air conditioning) system. A properly designed and functioning HVAC system (1) provides thermal comfort, (2) distributes adequate amounts of outdoor air to meet occupants' ventilation needs, and (3) removes odors and contaminants. An adequate and properly maintained HVAC system is an essential component of a healthy and comfortable environment.

General Ventilation Concepts

There are two basic types of ventilation—general and local. General ventilation deals with pollutants by supplying and exhausting large volumes of air throughout a building. Local ventilation controls contaminants by capturing them at or near the place they are generated and exhausting them directly outdoors. General ventilation works through the principle of dilution; local ventilation works through isolation and removal before a contaminant spreads throughout an occupied area (Clayton 1978).

To conserve energy, a percentage of the stale air that is exhausted from an occupied space is mixed with fresh outside air, cleaned, and recirculated. This supply air (outdoor air plus recirculated air) can be made up of various amounts of recirculated air (from 0 to 100%) and outside air (from 100 to 0%). Once mixed, this air is delivered by ducts to the appropriate spaces (Figure 3-1).

General Ventilation Method

There are many types or configurations of HVAC systems, but one of the most basic distinguishing features is the number of air-handling units (AHU). An AHU is a component of an HVAC system that includes a fan (to move the air) and filters and coils (to condi-

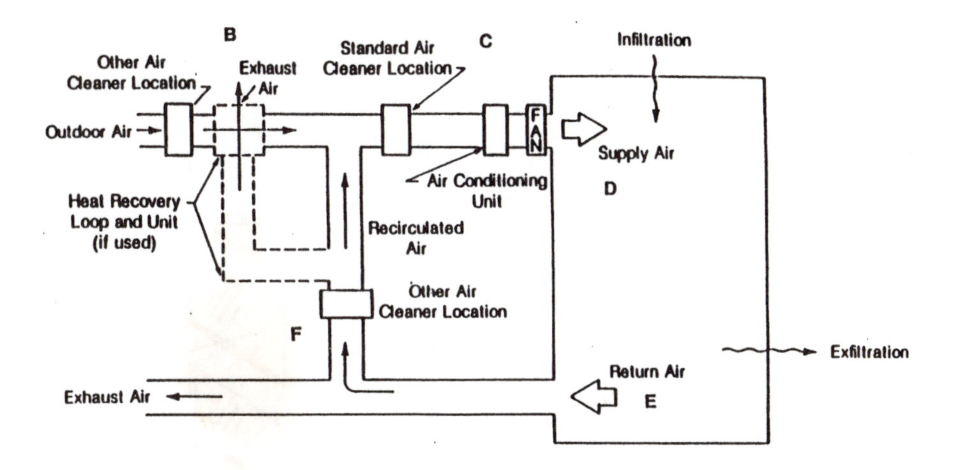

Figure 3-1. Schematic representation of a mechanical ventilation system. This figure is keyed to Figure 3-2 through common symbols A–F that show equivalent features of the system. [Reprinted from B. H. Turk et al. (1987), "Indoor air quality and ventilation measurements in 38 Pacific Northwest commercial buildings," Final Report to the Bonneville Power Administration, Lawrence Berkeley Laboratory Report No. LBL-23315.]

tion the air). In decentralized systems, numerous air-handling units service a building; in a centralized system, there is only one or just a few. Buildings can utilize a combination of these two approaches: combining a main centralized system that supplies air to occupants through ducts, and decentralized systems that deliver air directly to occupants.

In large office buildings, the AHU of a centralized ventilation system can occupy a whole floor. This central unit supplies air to all areas but usually employs two different systems to move the air—one system supplies air to the building's core, while a second system supplies air to the building perimeter. The perimeter units are called induction units; although they are part of the central system, they contain components of a decentralized AHU—that is, each induction unit has its own heating/cooling coil that permits adjusting the temperature.

The two systems differ in how the supply air is delivered to the occupant's space. With the core supply system, the supply fans feed horizontal ducts (located above the drop ceiling) that distribute the air to diffusers located throughout the interior. The location of the diffusers is extremely important since they dictate where air exits the duct. With the perimeter induction units, separate ducts from the central AHU connect to a distribution system located between the vertical columns along the perimeter wall. These ducts supply the perimeter units, which are usually located between the vertical columns and directly under a window. The perimeter units provide supply air from the wall of the building to about 15 feet inward. Both systems deliver the same supply air (outside plus return air), although the perimeter units have the added ability to heat or cool the air.

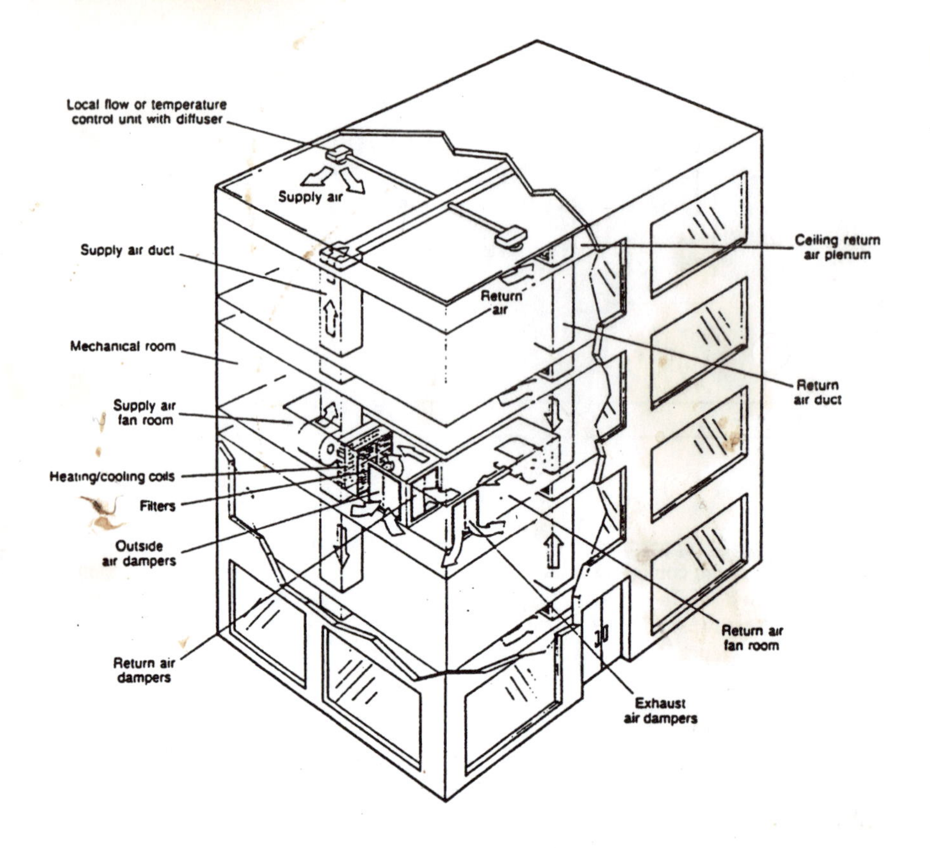

Figure 3-2. Pictorial representation of a typical mechanical ventilation system. This figure is keyed to Figure 3-1 through common symbols A–F that show equivalent features of the system. [Reprinted from B. H. Turk et al. (1987), "Indoor air quality and ventilation measurements in 38 Pacific Northwest commercial buildings," Final Report to the Bonneville Power Administration, Lawrence Berkeley Laboratory Report No. LBL-23315.]

Part of a centralized HVAC system is a return air system that can carry stale air from the occupied space back to a mixing chamber, either via ducts or by an "unducted" system—using the space between ceiling and the drop ceiling as a return air plenum. Ceiling plenums first became popular in the early 1970s as a cost-saving design feature and continue to be widely used (Figure 3-2).

Centralized HVAC systems use one of two basic procedures to regulate the flow of air to the occupants: (1) a constant air volume system (CAV) and/or (2) a variable air volume (VAV) system. CAV systems deliver a constant volume of supply air to occupants; the temperature of a space is maintained by varying the temperature of the supply air being delivered.

VAV systems vary the amount of supply air; temperature is maintained by changing the supply air flow, rather than by altering temperature. VAV systems became the preferred system in the 1970s because they conserve energy: once the temperature requirements of a space are met, a VAV system may shut down and stop introducing supply air. Since under these conditions the occupants receive little fresh air, ASHRAE 62-89 suggests a minimum amount of supply air at all times.

Another way to control the introduction of outside air is based on carbon dioxide (CO_2) concentrations produced by occupants' respiration. Such systems are especially useful when the density of people in a space varies dramatically over time, as in an airport with peak and quiet periods of activity (ASTM 1995). However, if there are other contaminants, such as chemical contaminants, besides occupants' bioeffluents, this may not be an appropriate method.

Air Balancing

The design of an air distribution system dictates how much outside air is brought into the building, where the supply air (outside air plus recirculated air) is distributed, and how much air is exhausted. However, to know how much and where the air is actually being distributed, one has to conduct flow measurements. The process of measuring the distribution of supply air and the amounts of exhausted air is called "air balancing." Air balancing is very tedious and difficult since every supply diffuser—and there may be hundreds of diffusers involved—must be evaluated for total air flow in cubic feet per minute. Because of the expense involved, building owners are reluctant to conduct the necessary tests. However, without such testing, it is difficult to know if the system is functioning as intended—and this is especially true if changes have been made to the system or building over time.

Many factors can cause a well-designed ventilation system to be out of balance. Because of temperature or draft problems, people may place an obstruction in the supply diffuser to reduce the amount of supply air; that supply air is then redirected to another supply diffuser and the system no longer functions as designed. Also, when a drop ceiling is used as a return air plenum—which is quite common—missing or out-of-place tiles may disrupt the original air pattern design.

Changes in occupant density or activities may be made without concern for ventilation, and the location of existing supply diffusers and return air grilles may no longer be appropriate. Without physical testing, it is difficult to know if the system is functioning as designed or if the controls are working properly.

Another issue when evaluating ventilation design is "ventilation effectiveness." Ventilation effectiveness is concerned with both the distribution of supply air throughout the building and the occupied space (ASHRAE 62-89). Inadequate mixing usually occurs when the supply air diffusers and return air grilles are in close proximity and/or when there are elevated supply temperatures and low discharge velocities (Godish 1996). Although poor mixing of supply and room air has been demonstrated in laboratory studies, there is conflicting information as to how often this actually occurs in occupied buildings. This condition may occur when heating a building, because the heated supply air tends to hug the ceiling and not mix properly (Fisk 1995).

THERMAL COMFORT

Thermal comfort is critical in determining the acceptability of an indoor environment. Thermal comfort is a function of several environmental factors acting in concert with personal comfort level. The environmental factors include air temperature, relative humidity, radiant temperature, and air velocity. ASHRAE's "Thermal Environmental Conditions for Human Occupancy" addresses these environmental factors (ASHRAE 55-92). This standard specifies conditions in which 80% or more of the occupants will find the environment thermally acceptable. The temperature ranges given for office workers assumes that the workers will be dressed differently for each season: winter, 71 degrees F is optimum with an operative range of 68–75 degrees F; summer, 76 degrees F is optimum with operative range of 70–78 degrees F (ASHRAE 55-92).

Even though the standard suggests an optimum summer temperature of 76 degrees F, research and field studies have concluded that temperatures above 72 degrees F are associated with increased SBS (Jaakola 1991). Although the cause of SBS is believed to be "multifactorial," it seems temperature can play not only a direct role in promoting discomfort, but also can accentuate the role of other factors such as VOCs (Molhave 1993).

Studies have shown that the correlation between warm air temperature and increased complaints about air quality becomes strongest at temperatures above 75 degrees F (Berglund 1989). Also, temperature variances of the occupants' physical environment—vertical and horizontal temperature differences and draft—can cause perceived IAQ problems (Wyon 1996, ASHRAE 55-92).

Occupants can have significant temperature-related complaints in buildings with nonopening, nonthermal windows if the ventilation design is not adequate. For example, in an older building with such windows, the HVAC system might not be able to deal with the thermal load produced by computers, printers, and other equipment.

In addition, buildings with large windows can have substantial solar heat gains or losses, depending on the season and the time of day. This can cause discomfort in varying areas on different sides of the building as the sun moves during the course of the day. The thermal requirements of a space will change dramatically, but since the temperature may be controlled by a single thermostat—which may not be located in the area undergoing changes—the room may have a substantial temperature gradient. However, buildings with thermal windows circumvent this problem to a large degree.

Humidity

It is assumed that low indoor air humidity will tend to dry the mucosa of upper airways and cause eye irritation and upper respiratory problems. In fact, indoor air humidity does not seem to be related to the complaints of dryness associated with SBS, since studies have shown no clear association between measured indoor air humidity and the prevalence of SBS (Sundell 1993). However, the sensation of dryness maybe an important indicator of poor indoor air quality, even though this sensation, which is usually associated with low humidity because normally it occurs in winter when the indoor humidity is low, seems to be caused by other issues, such as VOCs (Sundell 1993).

On the other hand, high humidity, levels in excess of 60%, can promote microbial growth that contributes to poor indoor air quality. ASHRAE 62-89R sets upper limits on humidity to help reduce moisture and subsequently retard microbial growth. This topic is discussed in the chapters on microbial contamination and pro-active techniques.

VENTILATION REQUIREMENTS

The ventilation needs of building occupants are met by supplying a sufficient amount of outdoor and recirculated air that has been conditioned (filtered, heated, or cooled and perhaps humidified). The amount of ventilation air supplied should be able to reduce bioeffluents and also reduce contaminants produced by occupants' activities and by emissions from interior furnishings.

However, ventilation standards originated with a concern for reducing odors from the bioeffluents produced from occupants (Yaglou 1936). ASHRAE's first ventilation standard (ASHRAE Standard 62-73) called for introducing enough fresh outside air to reduce contaminates and maintain a certain CO_2 level (see the chapter on history and evolution). The minimum outside air ventilation rate called for was 5 cfm per person, which results in a buildup of CO_2 that approaches 2500 parts per million (ppm).

When IAQ problems increased during the 1970s and 1980s, it was believed that the ventilation rate of 5 cfm per person might be inadequate for acceptable air quality (Kreiss 1984). ASHRAE responded by introducing a new standard, "Ventilation for Acceptable Indoor Air Quality—62-89," which increased the ventilation rate for office buildings from 5 to 20 cfm per person. The introduction of 20 cfm per person would result in a level of CO_2 under 1000 ppm and solve the bioeffluent odor problem.

The standard addresses odor and comfort vis-à-vis bioeffluents but does not discuss contaminates such as volatile organic emissions from building materials or occupants' activities.

Studies to evaluate the effect of different quantities of fresh air on occupant satisfaction/dissatisfaction have shown mixed results (Sundell 1994, Jaakola 1994). Although it would seem that the more fresh air brought into a building the better the air quality, this is not always the case. Ventilation rates up to 20 cfm seem to be beneficial, but levels in excess of 20 cfm have not been proved to be more acceptable (Godish 1996).

Ventilation Systems as Sources of Contaminants

Ventilation systems themselves can be a source of contaminants and also their distribution. Air conditioning—i.e., the cooling of air—is particularly problematic; there are more complaints about poor air quality in buildings with air conditioning than in those without air conditioning or those with natural ventilation (Zweers 1992). Cooling air below its dew point creates liquid water (condensate) and this moisture nurtures microbial growth on organic substrates, which can contribute to poor air quality (Morey 1988).

Building ventilation systems provide numerous areas for microbial growth and subsequent airborne distribution that warrant close observation. These include humidifiers containing reservoirs of stagnant water, induction units, filters, porous insulation in ventilation systems, and outdoor air intakes.

A common problem with perimeter induction units is an occupants' tendency to cover the tops of these units. This disrupts and alters the air patterns, resulting in unsatisfactory environmental conditions. Also, food materials are sometimes stored or placed on top of the units; the food can spill into the unit and become a source for microbial growth (discussed in chapters on microbial contamination and pro-active methods).

Microorganisms are only one of the contaminants HVAC systems can harbor and distribute; for instance, an HVAC system with a poorly designed filtration system might allow the accumulation and distribution of dirt. It is imperative that HVAC systems be designed to permit proper maintenance, which includes access to critical areas for inspection and cleaning.

SUMMARY

The intent of building design relative to IAQ is to achieve a comfortable environment in which the majority of occupants express no dissatisfaction. This requires: (1) supplying enough air to sufficiently reduce bioeffluents and building-related contaminants, (2) maintaining a temperature that is perceived to be acceptable, (3) limiting unwanted moisture and infiltration of unconditioned air into the building, and (4) curtailing the sources of VOCs (see chapters on VOCs and pro-active methods). A properly designed and maintained HVAC system is key to achieving these goals.

SUGGESTIONS FOR EVALUATION

- Discuss key points in how building design effects air quality.
- Define the various types of HVAC systems.
- Give an overview of ventilation requirements.
- Discuss the importance of temperature, humidity, and supply air distribution.

KEY WORDS AND CONCEPTS

General ventilation, local ventilation, CAVs, VAVs, ventilation effectiveness, ventilation requirements, pressure differential, building emissions, ASHRAE 62-89, ASHRAE 62-89R, demand-controlled ventilation, supply air, outside air, AHU

REFERENCES

ASHRAE Draft Standard 62-89R, "Ventilation for Acceptable Indoor Air Quality: Public Review Draft" (1996), ASHRAE, Atlanta.

ASHRAE Standard 55-92, "Thermal Environmental Conditions for Human Occupancy" (1992), ASHRAE, Atlanta.

ASTM, "Provisional Standard Guide for Using Indoor Carbon Dioxide Concentrations to Evaluate Indoor Air Quality and Ventilation" (1995), PS 40-95, West Conshocken, PA.

Bearg, D., *Indoor Air Quality and HVAC Systems* (1993), Lewis Publishers, Boca Raton.

Berglund, L. G., and Cain, W. S., *IAQ 88, The Human Equation: Health and Comfort* (1989), ASHRAE, Atlanta.

Clayton, G., and Clayton, F. (eds.), *Patty's Industrial Hygiene and Toxicology* (1978), third edition, Vol. 1, Wiley-Interscience, New York.

EPA *Code of Federal Regulations: National Primary and Secondary Ambient Air Quality Standards. 40 CFR part 50* (1994), Environmental Protection Agency, Washington.

Fanger, P. O., and Melikov, A. K. (1989), "Turbulence and Draft," *ASHRAE J.*, 31(4), Atlanta.

Fisk, W. J., Faulkner, D., Sullivan, D., and Baumann, F. (1995), "Air Change Effectiveness and Pollutant Removal Efficiency during Adverse Mixing Conditions," *Indoor Air*, Vol. 5.

Godish, T., and Spengler, J. D. (1996), "Relationships Between Ventilation and Indoor Air Quality: A Review," *Indoor Air*, 6:135–146.

Jaakola, J. J. K., Heinonen, O. P., and Seppanen, O. (1991), "Mechanical Ventilation of Office Buildings and Sick Building Syndrome. An Experimental and Epidemiological Study," *Indoor Air*, 1:111–121

Kreiss, K., and Hodgson, M. J., *Building Associated Epidemics: Indoor Air Quality* (1984), CRC Press, Boca Raton.

Molhave, L., Liu, Z., Jorgensen, A. H., Pedersen, O. F., and Kjaegaard, S. K. (1993), "Sensory and Physiological Effects on Humans of Combined Exposures to Air Temperatures and Volatile Organic Compounds," *Indoor Air,* 3:155–169.

Morey, P. R., "Microorganisms in Buildings and HVAC Systems: A Summary of 21 Environmental Studies," *Proceedings of IAQ'88:Engineering Solutions to Indoor Air Problems* (1988), ASHRAE, Atlanta.

Persily, A. K., "Assessing ventilation effectiveness in mechanically ventilated office buildings," *Proceedings of International Symposium on Room Air Convection and Ventilation Effectiveness* (1992), ASHRAE, Atlanta.

Singh, H. B. (ed.), *Composition, Chemistry and Climate of the Atmosphere* (1996), Van Nostrand Reinhold Books, New York.

Sundell, J., and Lindvall, T. (1993), "Indoor Air Humidity and Sensation of Dryness as Risk Indicators of SBS," *Indoor Air*, 6:382–393.

Wyon, D. P., and Sandberg, M. (1996), "Discomfort Due to Vertical Thermal Gradients," *Indoor Air*, 6:48–54.

Yaglou, C. P., Riley, E. C., and Coggins, D. I., "Ventilation Requirements" (1936), ASHRAE, *Transaction,* 42, Atlanta.

Zweers, T., Preller, L., Brunekreef, B., and Boleij, J. (1992), "Health and Indoor Climate Complaints of 2043 Office Workers in 61 Buildings in the Netherlands," *Indoor Air*, 2:127–136.

SUGGESTED READINGS

ASHRAE, *Handbook of Fundamentals I-P Edition* (1993), ASHRAE, Atlanta.

ASHRAE Standard 62-89, "Ventilation for Acceptable Indoor Air Quality" (1989), ASHRAE, Atlanta.

Bearg, D. *Indoor Air Quality and HVAC Systems* (1993), Lewis Publishers, Boca Raton.

Cone, J., and Hodgson, M. (eds.), *Problem Buildings: Building Associated Illness and the Sick Building Syndrome, Occupational Medicine: State of the Art Reviews* (1989), Hanley and Belfus, Philadelphia, 4(4).

EPA, "Building Air Quality: A Guide for Building Owners and Facility Managers" (1997), Superintendent of Documents, Pittsburgh.

Godish, T., *Sick Buildings* (1997), CRC Press, Boca Raton.

Persily, A. K., *Manual for Ventilation Assessment in Mechanically Ventilated Commercial Buildings* (1994), National Institute of Standards and Technology, NISTIR 5329, Gaithersburg, MD.

Trechsel, H. R., and Lagus, P. L. (eds.), *Measured Air Leakage of Buildings* (1986), ASTM, Philadelphia.

Chapter 4

VOLATILE ORGANIC COMPOUNDS

OVERVIEW

The past 50 years have seen a dramatic increase in the use of synthetic materials and chemicals that produce volatile organic compounds (VOCs). This chapter reviews the sources and levels of VOCs in the indoor environment and their relationship to the health and well-being of building occupants.

In general, indoor VOC levels in nonindustrial settings are so low they defy interpretation with occupational standards. Still, it is believed that they may play a significant role in building-related complaints, especially those concerning sensory irritation. Although the specific health implications are unclear for most VOCs, formaldehyde is known to be harmful and is therefore discussed in detail. Environmental tobacco smoke is not covered; the impact of these VOCs is well documented and it is assumed that buildings will be either smoke-free or have limited smoking areas.

This chapter also discusses emission characteristics and monitoring VOCs, but a more detailed look at monitoring is found in the chapter on investigations and evaluation techniques. Reducing VOC emissions is covered in the chapter on pro-active methods.

LEARNING OUTCOMES

- A knowledge of VOCs, their emission characteristics and sources
- A knowledge of VOCs and health issues
- A knowledge of formaldehyde (emission and health characteristics)

BACKGROUND

Organic compounds contain carbon atoms, which are unique in their ability to link and form chainlike or ring structures. A partial list of organic compounds includes petroleum products, perfumes, pesticides, plastics, synthetic fibers, refrigerants, dyes, pigments, and surface coatings (paints, adhesives, etc).

Organic compounds can be classified by their boiling points as very volatile, volatile, and semivolatile. The volatile organic compounds (VOCs), those with boiling points between 122 and 500 degrees F, have the most impact on indoor air quality (WHO 1986).

VOCs can be further differentiated by their chemical structure. They can be grouped into such major classes of organic compounds as aliphatic (straight chain compounds), alkylated aromatics (ring compounds), halogenated hydrocarbons (with chlorine and/or fluorine atoms), and oxygenated compounds.

VOC Emission Processes

Three fundamental processes control the rate of VOC emissions from building sources: (1) evaporation—for example, paint drying; (2) desorption of adsorbed compounds—for example, an organic residue left on a surface that gradually evaporates; and (3) diffusion within a material—for example, formaldehyde gas trapped in a product that slowly moves through the product and is released in the gaseous state when it reaches the surface (Tichenor 1989). How fast the VOCs are produced depends on the process and the source characteristics.

All three processes are significantly influenced by building parameters such as temperature, air exchange rate, and air velocity (Tichenor 1989). Because of all these variables, emissions rates will vary over time as will the resulting VOC concentrations in the air. Fluctuations in concentrations can be extremely variable, changing 3 to 4 orders of magnitude over a short period of time.

SIGNIFICANT SOURCES OF VOCs

The sources of VOCs are legion. Some of the most significant contributors of VOCs in an office environment include building materials and furnishings, building maintenance products, occupants' activities, equipment, and special processes such as printing operations or film processing. Studies have shown that materials and activities followed by ventilation systems were the most important sources of VOCs (Bluyssen 1996).

In general, emission characteristics for wet materials (adhesives, paints, etc.) are initially high, but decrease sharply during the first few hours after application. Dry materials (floor coverings, furnishings, ceiling materials, cubicles or desk dividers, etc.) typically off-gas a significant amount of VOCs during the first 60 days following manufacture. Building materials usually are the dominant source of VOCs for up to 12 months after construction (Wolkoff 1995).

Building materials and furnishings have a finite amount of VOCs to off-gas, as demonstrated by the decrease in VOCs with time after installation. Office equipment and occupants' activities, on the other hand, are a continuous source of VOCs; dry or wet process photocopying machines, laser and ink printers, fax machines, and paper handling are some ongoing sources of emissions.

VOCs can be adsorbed to and released from furnishings (Borazzo 1990). Thus, during a wet application such as painting, the high levels of VOCs released during the drying process can adhere to fleecy materials and off-gas at another time. This phenomenon—called a sink effect—is an important factor in determining exposure (Wallace 1991).

VOC CONCENTRATIONS

As noted, the emissions of VOCs from materials will vary with the age of the source, the type of VOC transfer process (evaporation, desorption, or diffusion), and the impact of environmental factors such as temperature, humidity, air changes, and air velocity. Because these factors are constantly changing, the concentrations will also change with time, and how dramatic that change is will depend on the circumstances. Therefore, when looking at VOC levels, it is important to know what factors and variables may have influenced the findings.

Given the variables, the information that can be gained by determining VOC levels at any one time is limited. With this in mind, studies have reported that concentrations of individual compounds in established settings are usually at the low parts per billion level with measurements below 50 micrograms per cubic meter ($\mu g/m^3$), with most below 5 $\mu g/m^3$ (Brown 1994). In buildings with such VOC sources as new materials or activities involving solvents, concentration can be higher by orders of magnitude (Brown 1994). Even at these higher concentrations, the concentrations would usually be in the low parts per billion (ppb) range if expressed in a volume per volume relationship.

TVOCs

Office buildings almost always contain a complex mixture of VOCs encompassing many different classes of organics. Therefore, a technique for summing them up and reporting them as one number is advantageous from a practical standard point (Molhave 1986). This has been done in the past by adding together the mass of organics measured in a sample and reporting the results as a total VOC (TVOC) level that is a summation of individual concentrations. Although this technique is easy to do, there are substantial limitations when relating the results to health issues. A European research team concluded "TVOC's cannot be used as a surrogate for the intensity or acceptability of any effects." Because of this, these researchers suggested eliminating the use of TVOC levels completely (Commission of the European Communities 1998).

Although use of the TVOC indicator for health and discomfort is questioned, the levels observed are useful as indicators of background levels of organics. For example, a European study reported the average TVOC concentrations in 54 buildings in 9 countries to be below 500 $\mu g/m^3$, with a few exceptions (Bluyssen 1995). Studies in this country found basically the same results. When the EPA studied the TVOC levels in 16 randomly selected buildings, the levels for the most part did not exceed 500 $\mu g/m^3$ (ASHRAE 1989-62R). A study of the literature from 1983—1993 revealed a TVOC range from 20 to 5300 $\mu g/m^3$ (Hoskins 1993). It should be noted that even the highest level observed—5300 $\mu g/m^3$—is only about 1 ppm.

INFLUENCE ON HEALTH

The health implications of low-level concentrations of most VOCs are, in general, not clear. Although certain symptoms have been proved to be associated with high VOC levels, it is difficult to document any correlation with low VOC levels. Also, an understanding of the etiology concerning low-level complex mixtures of VOCs with various problems are largely lacking or unclear. Formaldehyde, a VOC usually found in the indoor environment, is of special interest because its health implications at low levels have been documented (Hanna 1989). It is discussed below in a separate section.

Although the health implications of most VOCs are not clear, they are believed to contribute to complaints related to poor indoor air quality, such as those for sick building syndrome (SBS), where symptoms include headaches, fatigue, difficulty concentrating and irritability. Such symptoms also observed with exposure to VOCs in the industrial environment (Hodgson 1995). VOC levels in the office environment are very low and defy comparison with industrial levels. It must also be noted that industrial environments usually contain very high levels of one dominant VOC, whereas the nonindustrial environment usually has a complex mixture of VOCs at very low concentrations.

Industrial exposure standards are designed to protect workers from clinically definable adverse health effects. Industrial standards for individual VOCs are typically between the 1 to 100 ppm levels or 3000 to 300,000 $\mu g/m^3$ range. These levels are rarely seen in the office environment, and then only under the most unusual circumstances. For example, a VOC such as toluene, which is usually found in offices at concentrations of less than 50 $\mu g/m^3$, has an industrial health standard of 180,000 $\mu g/m^3$.

Moreover, concerns about low-level exposures usually arise around the perception of odor and irritation, and VOCs are considered to be only one of a combination of factors that cause such complaints. Studies of low levels of VOCs and sensory responses that involve odor, nasal pungency, and eye irritation show that mixtures of VOCs cause responses at concentrations far below what would be expected for each component of the mixture (Gammage 1996). It seems that increasing the number of VOCs in a complex mixture can lower the thresholds for odor as well as for eye and nasal irritation. Work is currently being done on a possible model to predict the irritation potency for individual compounds and mixtures.

Two different studies suggest yet another possible issue. One study of the complex mixture of VOCs at levels observed in new buildings used subjects who had previously reported "indoor climate symptoms" but were basically healthy. This study found indications of chemical changes in eye and nose liquids and also significant declines in performance, demonstrating that exposures to low levels of VOCs had an adverse effect on the ability to concentrate (Molhave 1991). When this experiment was repeated with healthy subjects having no history of discomfort related to the indoor environment, the VOCs caused headaches and general discomfort, but no effect on performance was documented (Otto 1992).

These two studies suggest that some people may be more susceptible to SBS, with a lower threshold for certain effects. A study of physiological and psychological characteristics associated with low levels of VOCs states "to deal with the finding of illness from nontoxic levels of chemicals, it is necessary to study the person who feels ill in interactions with the environment rather than the environment alone" (Bell 1990).

Similarity, the European Audit Project, with researchers from 16 European institutions involving 11 countries, concluded there is great variability in how individuals respond to environmental conditions, including VOCs. The project reported that a large number of subjects would be needed in any study in order to reduce the confounding effect of individual variability, noting that to date most studies have used relatively small numbers of subjects with conflicting results—some studies show a response to low levels of VOCs, some show no response (Bluyssen 1995).

Formaldehyde

Formaldehyde, one of the most widely produced chemicals and used primarily as an adhesive in pressed wood products and urea-formaldehyde foam insulation (UFFI), is not only irritating to the mucous membranes but is a primary skin sensitizing agent inducing allergic contact dermatitis. Dose-effect studies have shown that exposure to low levels of formaldehyde produces irritancy problems and behavioral changes. Formaldehyde has also been associated with severe hypersensitive reactions in nonindustrial settings such as schools (Hanna 1990).

Formaldehyde has been associated primarily with poor indoor air quality in residential settings such as mobile homes and houses with UFFI. Office buildings, however, do not have a significant amount of formaldehyde-containing material relative to their volume of air (Girman 1989). Moreover, because of health concerns, the use of pressed-wood products (e.g., plywood) and other sources of formaldehyde have substantially decreased in the last 10 years.

However, recently it was discovered that formaldehyde could be produced by reactions involving other VOCs and indoor sources of ozone (Weschler 1992). Low levels of ozone, produced by office equipment such as photocopiers, react with various VOCs to form formaldehyde. Studies have shown VOCs other than formaldehyde were reduced substantially by reacting with ozone, but formaldehyde levels were increased greatly. In essence, less harmful VOCs react to form the more toxic compound formaldehyde.

MEASUREMENT TECHNIQUES

When sampling for VOCs in an industrial setting, the following is usually applicable: the VOC or VOCs to be measured are known, the concentrations are in the parts per million range, the source is constant or at least predictable, and any process changes are documentable. In such structures, there are recommended sampling and analytical procedures.

The situation in nonindustrial settings is rarely as clear cut, and such settings may contain hundreds of low-level VOCs with different chemical characteristics. Therefore, any sampling/analytical technique must be applicable for a mixture of VOCs that may have a wide range of chemical characteristics and be sensitive enough to measure in the parts per billion range (Wolkoff 1995). Also, emission sources and building conditions are constantly changing, which will greatly influence the levels.

There are techniques for measuring low levels of individual VOCs and TVOCs that address some of these issues (Wolkoff 1995). However, there is no consensus on sampling techniques or data interpretation. The various testing strategies and their advantages and disadvantages are discussed in the chapter on diagnosing IAQ problems.

VOC EXPOSURE STANDARDS

To date, the only United States exposure standards for individual VOCs are occupational exposure standards such as threshold limit values (TLVs) and permissible exposure limits (PELs). However, Canada does have a nonindustrial standard of 0.1 ppm for formaldehyde, and the World Health Organization suggests a nonindustrial level of 0.08 ppm. In contrast, the United States has an industrial exposure standard (PEL) only for formaldehyde, which is 0.75 ppm.

As noted in the chapter on building-associated illness, the industrial standards apply to situations where the concentrations are much higher than in offices, and the adverse health effects include documentable clinical abnormalities. In addition, industrial standards are intended to protect a healthy worker from individual compounds in an industrial environment.

In general, a VOC standard for office environments would have to be designed to protect all workers (even susceptible people) from a complex mixture of low levels of VOCs, even though there is presently no clear documentation of the connection between VOCs and health. At this time, except for formaldehyde, it is impossible to predict human sensory response for the low levels of the complex VOC mixtures usually observed.

Recently, the Danish National Institute of Occupational Health issued guidelines for 26 different compounds (Nielsen 1998). These guidelines include odor, sensory irritation of the eyes and upper respiratory tract, lower respiratory tract irritation, and systemic effects. The levels recommended varied in range from 1/40 to 1/4 of recognized health standards.

There have been attempts to use TVOC levels to determine exposure standards, but as noted earlier in this chapter, associations between TVOC concentrations and health effects are unclear (Commission of the European Communities 1998). One major problem is that using a TVOC level assumes that each VOC in that mixture is equally important in relation to health, but in fact, one VOC may be more hazardous than others.

Molhave has suggested that irritation is unlikely if TVOC concentrations are below 0.2 mg/m^3 and is likely if concentration are above 3 mg/m^3 (Molhave 1991). Gammage has suggested using 5 mg/m^3 of TVOCs as an "action level," meaning the level at which one takes more definitive organic measurements, tries to locate and remove the strongest sources of VOCs, and increases ventilation to dilute the airborne VOCs (Gammage 1989).

A technique to evaluate data without using numerical standards would be to review the compounds/concentrations in terms of differences observed (e.g., temporal, spatial, activities, renovations, constructions, etc.). Studies have shown that although mean concentrations of individual compounds in established settings are usually quite low, activities in buildings involving sources of VOCs can influence concentrations by orders of magnitude; thus, decision-making based on interpretation of the data is difficult, but various comparisons may help (Brown 1994).

Currently, even though there is no consensus on any numerical standards for VOCs, other than formaldehyde in nonindustrial settings, it is believed advisable to keep VOC levels as low as possible. Guidelines for limiting the introduction of VOCs in buildings through source control are discussed in the chapter on pro-active techniques.

SUMMARY

The dramatic increase in synthetic materials and chemicals in nonindustrial complexes has resulted in elevated levels of a complex mixture of VOCs. Although the levels are higher than those found in outdoor air, the concentrations are far below industrial levels.

The sources of VOCs are legion, but the most significant VOCs sources are building materials and furnishings, building maintenance products, occupants' activities, equipment, and special processes. During a structure's first 12 months, building materials and furnishings are one of the major sources of VOCs, but emissions from office equipment and occupants' activities are a continuous source. Whatever the source, emission rates tend to fluctuate greatly and can be influenced substantially by such factors as temperature, air exchange rate, and air velocity. There is currently no consensus on sampling strategies or on how to interpret the data collected. Nonetheless, a pro-active approach of reducing all VOCs is recommended.

VOCs are believed to contribute to complaints related to poor air quality such as irritation and other SBS problems. Although the negative impact of lowlevels of complex mixtures of VOCs is unclear, the toxic nature of low levels of formaldehyde has been well documented.

SUGGESTIONS FOR EVALUATION

- List major sources of VOCs.
- Define the three emission processes for building materials.
- Discuss the effects of the environment on VOC emissions.
- Discuss VOC concentrations and the problems with measuring them.
- Discuss the health implications of low levels of VOCs, including formaldehyde.

KEY CONCEPTS AND WORDS

VOCs, TVOCs, formaldehyde, evaporation, desorption, diffusion, emission rates, concentrations, PELs, TLVs, sensory irritation, sink effect

REFERENCES

ASHRAE Draft Standard 62-89R, "Ventilation for Acceptable Indoor Air Quality: Public Review Draft" (1996), ASHRAE, Atlanta.

Bell, I. (1990), "The Biopersonality of Allergies and Environmental Illness," Eighth Annual International Symposium of Man and His Environment in Health and Disease, Dallas.

Bluyssen, P. M., Fernandes, E. O., Fanger, P. O., Groes, L., Clausen, G., Roulet, C., Bernard, C. A., and Valbjorn, O., *Final Report, European Audit Project to Optimize Indoor Air Quality and Energy Consumption in Office Buildings* (1995), TNO Building Construction Research, The Netherlands.

Brown, S. K, Sim, M. R., Abramson, M. J., Gray, C. N. (1994), "Concentrations of Volatile Organic Compounds in Indoor Air—A Review," *Indoor Air*, 3(2), 123–134.

Calabrese, E. J., and Kenyon, E. M., *Air Toxics and Risk Assessment* (1991), Lewis Publishers, Chelsea, MI.

Cain, W. S., and Cometto-Muniz, J. E., "Irritation and Odor: Symptoms of Indoor Air Pollution" (1993), *Proceedings of Indoor Air '93*, Helsinki, Finland (1), 561–565.

Commission of the European Communities (1998), "ECA-IAQ, Total Volatile Organic Compounds (TVOC) in Indoor Air Quality Investigations," Report 19 (eur17675 EN), Ispra, Italy.

Gammage, R. B., Hansen, D. L., and Johnson, L. W. (1989), "Indoor Air Quality Investigations: A Practitioner's Approach," *Environment International,* 15:503–510.

Gammage, R. B., and Berven, B. A. (eds.), *Indoor Air and Human Health* (1996), Lewis Publishers, Boca Raton.

Girman, J., "Volatile Organic Compounds and Building Bake-out." In Cone, J., and Hodgson, M. (eds.), Problem Buildings: State of the Art Reviews in Occupational Medicine (1989), Hanley and Belfus Publishers, Philadelphia.

Hanna, W. T., Painter, P. C., and Gammage, R. B., "Unusual Hypersensitive Reaction in Girls at a School with Urea-Formaldehyde Insulation," *The Practitioner's Approach to Indoor Air Quality Investigations* (1990), American Industrial Hygiene Association, Fairfax, VA, 19–35.

Hodgson, A. T. (1995), "A Review and a Limited Comparison of Methods for Measuring Total Volatile Organic Compounds in Indoor Air," *Indoor Air*, 5(4): 247–257.

Hoskins, J. A., Brown, R. C., and Levy, L. S., "The Construction and Evaluation of a Data-Base of Indoor Air Pollutants: VOCs" (1993), *Proceedings of Indoor Air '93*, Helsinki, (2) 57–63.

Molhave, L. (1991), "Volatile Organic Compounds, Indoor Air Quality and Health," *Indoor Air*, 4:357–376.

Nielsen, G. D. (1998) "Toxicological Based Air Quality Guidelines for Substances in Indoor Air," *Indoor Air*, Supplement 5.

Otto, D. A, Hudnell, H. K., House, D. E., Molhave, L., and Counts, W., "Exposure of Humans to a Volatile Organic Mixture" (1992) *Arch. Environ. Health*, 47.

Roberts, J. D., and Caserio M. C., *Basic Principles of Organic Chemistry* (1965), W. A. Benjamin, Inc., New York.

Samimi, B., "Assessment of Emission of Formaldehyde from Wood Products in Homes" (1996), Presented at AIHCE, Washington, D.C.

Tichenor, B. A., "Indoor Air Sources: Using Small Environmental Test Chambers to Characterize Organic Emissions from Indoor Materials and Products" (1989), EPA-600/8-89-074, Research Triangle Park, NC.

Wallace, L., Pellizzari, E., and Wendel, C., "Total Organic Concentrations in 2500 Personnel, Indoor and Outdoor Samples Collected in the US EPA TEAM Studies" (1990), *Proceedings of Indoor Air '90*, Canada Mortgage and Housing Corporation, Vol. 2, Ottawa.

Weschler, C. J., Hodgson, A. T., and Wooley, J. D. (1992), "Indoor Chemistry: Ozone, Volatile Organic Compounds, and Carpets," *Environmental Science Technology*, 26:2371–2377.

WHO (1986), "Indoor Air Quality Research," *World Health Organization*, Copenhagen, pp. 1–64.

Winberry, W. T., Forehand, L., Murphy, N. T., Ceroli, A., Phinney, B., and Evans, A., *Methods for Determination of Indoor Air Pollutants-EPA Methods* (1993), Noyes Data Corporation, Park Ridge, NJ.

Wolkoff, P. (1995), "Volatile Organic Compounds–Sources, Measurements, Emissions, and the Impact on Indoor Air Quality," *Indoor Air*, Supplement 3.

SUGGESTED READINGS

ASHRAE Draft Standard 62-89R, "Ventilation for Acceptable Indoor Air Quality: Public Review Draft" (1996), ASHRAE, Atlanta.

Cone, J., and Hodgsen, M. (eds.), *Problem Buildings: Building Associated Illness and the Sick Building Syndrome Occupational Medicine: State of the Art Reviews* (1989), Hanley and Belfus, Philadelphia, 4(4).

Gammage, R. B., and Berven, B. A. (eds.), *Indoor Air and Human Health* (1996), Lewis Publishers, Boca Raton.

Godish, T., *Sick Buildings* (1996), CRC Press, Boca Raton.

Nielsen, G. D. (1998), "Toxicological Based Air Quality Guidelines for Substances in Indoor Air," *Indoor Air*, Supplement 5.

Wolkoff, P. (1995), "Volatile Organic Compounds—Sources, Measurements, Emissions, and the Impact on Indoor Air Quality," *Indoor Air*, Supplement 3.

Chapter 5
MICROBIAL CONTAMINATION

OVERVIEW

The majority of building-related illnesses are thought to be caused by bioaerosols, which are airborne particles of microbial matter. These bioaerosols are more likely to affect people with a genetic predisposition for allergic problems.

Under normal circumstances, the number of microbes indoors is about the same as or less than that found outdoors. However, buildings can provide all the essentials for microbial growth, such as nutrients and moisture. The most crucial factor for microbial growth is moisture, which regulates the amount of growth as well as type of microbes that will proliferate.

For microorganisms to become a health issue they must be disseminated into the air (i.e., become aerosolized) and inhaled. One of the major causes of microbial amplification and distribution is HVAC systems.

Conducting bioaerosol risk assessments is extremely difficult because of the complexity of bioaerosols, the variety of health effects they produce, the fact that they usually affect only people with compromised immune systems, and the lack of guidelines and sampling protocols.

INTRODUCTION

Microorganisms such as bacteria and fungi are a normal and essential component of our ecosystem. They can live and grow in living organic material, nonliving organic material, or both. Saprophytic microorganisms, which include most fungi and many bacteria and protozoa, prefer nonliving organic material such as dead plant materials (ACGIH 1989). Parasitic microorganisms need a living host to grow. Saprophytic microorganisms are the most prevalent in the indoor environment because of their ability to find nourishment from nonliving matter; they are also the most important in terms of health effects because of their dominance.

Buildings can provide all the essentials for microbial growth because they contain many biodegradable materials. (Any material that can be decayed by microorganisms and thus support microbial growth is considered biodegradable. Biodegradable materials must contain carbon, nitrogen, sulfur, and phosphorus for microbial growth.)

Buildings can be constructed of or contain biodegradable material and/or provide sufficient nutrients through the introduction of outside dirt.

The wide variety of nutrients normally found outdoors encourages the growth of numerous different species. In addition, the "great outdoors" provides a dilution factor. Very rarely are significant concentrations of ambient biomatter found, except under certain conditions such as pollen season.

The indoor environment, on the other hand, generally provides an environment made up of select biodegradable construction materials and furnishings that tend to support specific species. Thus only certain microorganisms that enter a building from the outdoors will be encouraged to grow. In some cases, the type that comes to predominate may be particularly harmful.

Microbial growth can occur in the temperature range of less than 10 degrees C to greater than 50 degrees C (Nevalainen 1993). Building temperatures may enhance or deter microbial growth, but most microorganisms can grow at temperatures either below or above their optimum growth temperature.

The presence of nutrients and an acceptable temperature range are not sufficient to promote microbial growth; the most crucial prerequisite is moisture. Moisture not only regulates microbial growth, but the amount of moisture available dictates what type of microbes will proliferate (Nevalainen 1993). This is the major reason that one species will predominate in the indoor environment, whereas the outside environment usually does not encourage such selection.

Buildings, especially those with HVAC systems, are an excellent source of moisture. HVAC systems contain water reservoirs, humidifiers, or cooling towers, and they also have the potential to provide additional sources of moisture because of condensation, leaks, or floods (ASHRAE 62-89R).

When moisture is depleted and drying of the microbial mass occurs, microbial growth will decline. However, both fungal and bacterial spores can survive under dry conditions for years and blossom with the advent of moisture (Coggins 1991).

For microorganisms to become a health issue in a building, they must be disseminated into the air (i.e., become aerosolized) and inhaled by occupants.

SOURCES OF MOISTURE FOR GROWTH

Standing Water

As noted, moisture is crucial to microbial growth. Standing water can support most saprophytic microorganisms if it contains sufficient nutrients (i.e., organic material such as dirt or even dead microorganisms) and it is not depleted of oxygen. Water can accumulate where there is condensation, flooding, or leakage. Frequently there is pooling of water because of poor housecleaning or accidental flooding, such as a slop-sink overrunning or the wetting of a carpet around a watercooler. Water-damaged materials such as ceiling tiles may appear dry, but they contain sufficient moisture for microbial growth to occur.

HVAC Systems

HVAC systems play a crucial role in promoting moisture in buildings. In fact, HVAC systems are notorious for amplifying microbial growth and distributing microorganisms. One reason is that HVAC systems use water as part of their system (e.g., cooling towers and chill water); in addition, the cooling mode promotes condensation throughout the distribution system. Also, many components of an HVAC system can be a source of the moisture that is essential for microbial growth. These components include outdoor air inlets that trap moisture, dehumidifying cooling coils that reduce the temperature of moisture-laden air and subsequently form condensate, humidifiers that emit water droplets into the air from a reservoir of water, and porous insulation material that has become wet.

In essence, an HVAC system provides a perfect breeding ground—sufficient moisture, porous insulation material covered with a layer of organic material (dirt), as well as a distribution system (ducting) to aerosolize and disseminate the microbial growth (Foards 1996). In fact, dirt accumulated on uninsulated metal ventilation ducts will produce fungal growth with sufficient moisture (Pasanen 1993).

Since there is limited access to enclosed HVAC systems, visual assessment to observe microbial growth is difficult. The problem of microbial amplification in HVAC systems is generally ignored unless there is a rash of building-associated illnesses that is attributed to the environment. A program for proper HVAC inspection and maintenance is discussed in the chapter on pro-active techniques.

Materials

More than 40 years ago, researchers found that fungi obtain necessary moisture for growth not directly from atmospheric moisture but from substrates that absorb moisture from the environment (Block 1953). A relative humidity above 70% is considered a sufficient source of such moisture because it produces condensation or provides moisture that is subsequently adsorbed by hygroscopic (affinity for water) materials. Microbes are capable of using this adsorbed moisture for growth.

Relative humidity below 70% can also be an issue. If, for instance, a wall or duct is cooler than the indoor air, the relative humidity of the air surrounding that material will be higher, perhaps high enough to become a source of moisture for hygroscopic materials

Certain building materials are themselves a source of moisture. Even in the absence of an external source of moisture (e.g., condensation, leakage, etc.), these materials house free water held by adsorptive forces in the capillary spaces and on the surface (Flannigan 1996). The availability of this moisture for microbes is defined in terms of water activity.

Water activity (Aw) is defined as the ratio of the vapor pressure exerted by water in the material to the vapor pressure of pure water. Aw is an indication of the material's ability to support microbial growth—the higher the Aw the more moisture available. For example, an Aw in excess of 0.9 will encourage growth of microorganisms that require a lot of moisture; an Aw below 0.8, will support only microorganisms that are xerophilic, i.e., those needing very little moisture (Flannigan 1996).

Numerous studies have been conducted on the moisture requirements of microorganisms in terms of water activity. This can be of great importance in designing buildings with materials that do not enhance microbial growth and will be discussed in the chapter on pro-active techniques.

INFLUENCE OF MICROORGANISMS ON HEALTH

Excess microbial growth is associated with a variety of health problems, but the undisturbed presence of biomatter in a building in and of itself does not cause illness: two other conditions must occur. First, the biomatter has to become airborne (that is, aerosolized) and disseminated. Dissemination can be through any activity that disturbs the biomatter, but mechanical ventilation systems play an especially important role because such systems can distribute the biocontaminants throughout a building. In addition, the aerosolized biomatter must be inhaled to cause problems. Thus, the most significant health effects occur in the respiratory system, especially the lungs.

One response to the inhalation of either the microbes or their by-products is an allergic reaction. Other illnesses that may result include a variety of infections or diseases as well as irritation of respiratory mucosa, skin, and eyes.

Two major factors determine whether an organism will cause a disease (Burge 1990). The first factor is virulence—the capability of an organism to grow, reproduce, and cause infection. The second factor is immunity—a healthy person can usually ward off most virulent diseases, but someone with a weakened immune system is much more susceptible when exposed (Burge 1990). Individual response is particularly germane in the case of allergic reactions; one individual may experience an allergic reaction to a substance that leaves others unaffected. Individuals with a genetic predisposition to such allergic responses are called atopic.

In all cases, the response to aerosolized biomatter causes physical changes in the body that can be clinically monitored. This is the essential distinction between building-related illness and sick building syndrome. With sick building syndrome there is no physical abnormality that can be measured.

Allergic Diseases

The function of the immune system is to recognize "foreign" proteins (called antigens) and to form antibodies (also called immunoglobulin), as part of the body's defense against infection and disease (Clayman 1989). Microorganisms and/or their by-products can act as antigens and cause various allergic reactions. Allergies are inappropriate or exaggerated reactions of the immune system to foreign proteins, which may not actually be harmful; these reactions are termed hypersensitivity reactions.

Allergic reactions do not occur during the first exposure to an antigen. Rather, they occur only on the second or subsequent exposures to the biomatter, after the first contact has sensitized the body (Clayman 1989). During the first exposure, the antigens (in this case microbial material) provoke the immune system to produce specific antibodies, namely, immunoglobulin E or G. These antibodies coat the mast cells present in the stomach, lungs, and upper respiratory airways. At this first exposure, the person may not experience any ill effects, but when the antigen is encountered again, it binds to the antibodies and causes the mast cells to release chemicals that produce the allergic response (Clayman 1989). Allergic responses to aerosolized microbial matter include hypersensitivity pneumonitis, asthma, and rhinitis (hay fever) as well as mucous membrane irritation and chronic bronchitis.

Hypersensitivity pneumonitis (HP) causes fever, chills, and cough 8 to 12 hours after exposure. These symptoms disappear after one or two days but reappear after another exposure. Once an individual develops a sensitization of the respiratory tract, continued exposure to the antigen can lead to permanent disease. However, it is unclear how long the latency period is between exposure and onset of symptoms. Both atopic (a predisposition to various allergic reactions) and nonatopic occupants can get HP from exposure to specific organisms. There are numerous case studies of building-related HP outbreaks due to exposure and subsequent sensitization to microbial aerosols (Rose 1996).

In the United States alone it is estimated that more than 10 million people suffer from asthma. There are two main types of asthma: extrinsic, in which an allergy to an external factor triggers an attack, and intrinsic, in which there is no apparent external cause (Clayman 1989). The main symptoms are breathlessness, wheezing, a dry cough, and a feeling of tightness in the chest.

Allergic asthma and rhinitis (hay fever) can be caused by airborne fungus spores (ASHRAE 1989). But it is difficult to ascertain if a building-related source of microbial matter is in fact causing the asthma, because numerous other factors such as chemical irritants and cold air can induce asthma.

Microbial Agents

Some of the most common microbial agents that possess biological potency that cause disease are bacterial endotoxins, (1-3)-β-D-glucan, and mycotoxins (Rylander 1992).

Endotoxins are compounds found in the outer cell wall of gram negative bacteria (commonly found in the indoor environment); they cause inflammation of the lung and also affect the immune system (Rylander 1992). Elevated endotoxin levels are associated with mist from ultrasonic and other "cool mist" humidifiers (Milton 1996). Such humidification systems are routinely used in office buildings.

Another specific agent that can be found in bioaerosols is (1-3)-β-D-glucan. This compound is found in the cell-wall structure of fungi and some bacteria and affects the immune system.

Mycotoxins, large organic molecules produced by the fungal digestive process, can be extremely toxic. Mycotoxins have been primarily associated with mold contamination of cereals and grains. The most common fungi involved in producing the toxins that cause mycotoxicosis are *Fusarium, Aspergillus,* and *Penicillium* (Godish 1995).

Dust Mites

Although dust mites are a member of the spider family and not a microorganism, their body parts and fecal fragments can cause respiratory allergy. Dust mite allergens can cause allergic rhinitis, conjunctivitis, asthma, and dermatitis in sensitized individuals. Dust mites were formerly considered to be a problem only in homes, but they are now considered to be a potential problem in office complexes as well. An office environment provides the necessities for dust mite growth, such as skin cells for nutrients, humidity in excess of 45%, and a temperature between 65 and 80 degrees F. Office dust will contain some dust mites and upholstered chairs, which receive less maintenance than rugs and other potential sources, tend to collect human dander (Janko 1995).

Diseases—Transmission from Person to Person

Most viral and some bacterial diseases related to the indoor environment are transmitted from person to person, with individuals acting as reservoir, amplifier, and disseminator. In such cases, the disease-causing virus or bacteria is parasitic because it occurs in a living person. When the infected person sneezes or coughs, the aerosol produced carries the infectious material to another occupant, who may then become a host. Exposure to tuberculosis occurs this way, with the building enclosing the infectious agents and allowing the concentration to increase. Other diseases linked to human-to-human air transmission are influenza, the common cold, measles, rubella, and chicken pox.

Disease—Environmental Transmission

Some diseases are transmitted by environmental factors, rather than person to person. Environmental-source diseases include bacterial pneumonia and fungal infections (Burge 1990). The most infamous recent incident of such transmission was the 1976 Legionnaires' disease outbreak in Philadelphia, an event that prompted major concern for microbial hazards in nonindustrial environments. The *Legionella* bacterium causes both Legionnaires' disease and Pontiac Fever (see Chapter 2). Legionnaires' disease, the more serious, causes pneumonia, with fatality resulting about 15% of the time. The Centers for Disease Control estimates that 10,000 to 15,000 cases of Legionnaires' disease occur each year in the United States.

As previously mentioned, it is usually difficult to show cause and effect with environmental microbial exposures. Legionnaires' disease is an exception, in that cause and effect have been proved, although the transmission route may be complex. *Legionella* requires water, and the disease cannot occur in the absence of a contaminated water source. However, the mere presence of *Legionella* will not cause disease. The *Legionella*-contaminated water must be aerosolized and transported to the receptor before the disease legionellosis can occur (CDC 1999).

One study, for example, found the bacterium *Legionella* being amplified in an HVAC cooling tower, transmitted to a nearby hospital as aerosolized droplets (laden with bacteria), and causing Legionnaires' disease among the patients (Garbe 1985). Keeping the importance of the immunity factor in mind, it is worth noting people that the people who became ill were already hospitalized, with their health compromised.

RISK ASSESSMENT

Building-related illnesses are not that common, since the following conditions have to exist: (1) biomatter must be virulent, airborne, and in sufficient concentration to cause disease; (2) the biomatter must be inhaled by a building occupant with an immune system incapable of preventing subsequent illness.

To date, there is very little exposure data to demonstrate that a specific exposure (concentration and type) can cause a disease (Burge 1996). Burge notes, "one would like to see statistically relevant proof that exposure to a particular biological agent actually causes disease and such proof is generally not available for most bioaerosol-related diseases" (Burge 1989). Most of the time, the realization that building-related microbial matter may be implicated is anecdotal. If, for example, a source of microbial matter is found after illness occurs, it may be suspected as the cause of the illness.

A medical evaluation with a complete occupational and environmental exposure history, with attention to time spent in the office and any associated health issues, is necessary to make the correlation between a specific exposure and illness. This type of investigation happens infrequently. Also, a sick individual is probably not aware of a specific exposure, and to determine what biomatter is causing a health issue is extremely difficult. Even if the microbial exposure (i.e., type and concentration) is documented, laboratory data correlating the exposure with clinical abnormalities does not exist. Moreover, the resulting disease usually does not occur in large numbers of people, making a discovery of the cause/effect relationship between the building environment and the disease difficult for both patient and treating physician. The microbial source of the antigen is often not discovered, and in fact, it may not come from the patient's work environment.

STANDARDS AND GUIDELINES

As previously noted, risk assessment is difficult. Factors that contribute to the difficulty include the complexity of bioaerosols, the variety of health effects, the lack of background data for comparison purposes, and the lack of standardized protocols for assessing risk (Burge 1990).

In the absence of illness, numerical levels of viable microorganisms to define the sanitary conditions and the buildings environment have been suggested. A level of 500 colony-forming units per cubic meter has been proposed as a guideline, with the recommendation that any major differences in concentrations be noted and that outdoor sampling for comparative purposes be included (Gammage 1989).

The following health guidelines have been suggested for fungi in indoor air: (1) some fungi are unacceptable in indoor air; (2) colony-forming units per cubic meter (CFU/m^3) in excess of 50 are of concern if there is only one species present; (3) CFU/m^3 values less than 150 are acceptable if there is a mixture of species other than pathogens; and (4) CFU/m^3 value less than 300 are acceptable if the species are mainly *Cladosporium* (Miller 1988). Since there is no consensus on a standard, risk assessment is basically limited to a subjective examination of an environment for sources of microbial amplification. It is helpful to do comparison studies (e.g., outdoors versus indoors, variations in occupants' activities, changes in the ventilation system, problem areas versus problem-free areas). In any case, absolute numbers may be misleading. For example, samples from two areas may have the same total CFM/m^3, but one area may have a predominance of one species and the other area may have no predominant species. In another instance, the concentration may be low but the predominant species may be especially dangerous.

MEASUREMENTS

There is no one sampling protocol that applies to all types of bioaerosols, so the sampling technique must be dictated by the reason for sampling. Identification of biomatter is a highly skilled and arduous task that very few laboratories are capable of conducting. Still, sampling may be a useful tool in characterizing a previously located source, but the protocol must generate data that specifically addresses a purpose, or interpretation will be difficult. For example, sampling for bioaerosols can confirm the presence of *Legionella* bacteria in a cooling tower. In this case, the purpose of the sampling is well defined. Similarly, sampling can confirm that a preventive maintenance program involving the application of a biocide is working. With *Legionella*, the best way to characterize the potential for exposure would be to sample the cooling tower water and not the air for *Legionella*. However, even this type of sampling has its limitations. For example, studies have shown that protozoa ingest *Legionella* bacteria and the bacteria grow inside the protozoa. The levels of *Legionella* found in the cooling water may at this time may be considered low. However, when the protozoa dies, the *Legionella* is released and the levels will increase significantly (Barbaree 1986).

SUMMARY

All microorganisms contain or produce substances that can cause health problems. Materials of microbial origin are always present in a building, and given the opportunity, these materials can multiply, become airborne, and cause health problems.

A building has all the essentials for microbial growth (i.e., moisture and nutrients), along with a mechanical system to aerosolize biomatter and distribute it throughout the building. Aerosolizing the biomatter is crucial for promoting building-associated diseases such as hypersensitivity diseases. Hypersensitivity diseases that are known to result from exposure to airborne biomatter include hypersensitivity pneumonitis, allergic asthma, and allergic rhinitis.

An inherent difficulty in conducting any kind of bioaerosol risk assessment is the complexity of biomatter and the lack of recognized exposure standards. In addition, an individual's genetic predisposition will be a significant factor in determining if microbial matter will cause disease.

SUGGESTIONS FOR EVALUATION

- What do microorganisms need to proliferate and how do buildings provide them?
- Define the health issues associated with bioaerosols.
- Why is cause/effect from microbial exposures so difficult to evaluate?

KEY CONCEPTS AND WORDS

Bioaerosols, allergic reactions, hypersensitivity reactions, endotoxins, mycotoxins, nutrients, moisture, HVAC system, hypersensitivity pneumonitis, Legionella, dust mites, CFU/m^3, standing water

REFERENCES

ACGIH Committee on Bioaersols, *Guidelines for the Assessment of Bioaerosols in the Indoor Environment* (1989), ACGIH, Cincinnati.

Barbaree, J. M., Fields, B. S., and Feeley, J. C. (1986), "Isolation of Protozoa from Water Associated with a Legionellosis Outbreak and Demonstration of Intracellular Multiplication of Legionella pneumophila," *Appl. Environ. Microbiol.*, Feb., 422–424.

Block, S. S. (1953), *Appl. Microbiol.*, 1:287–293.

Burge, H. A. (1990), "Bioaerosols: Prevalence and Health Effects in the Indoor Environment," *Allergy Clin. Immunol.*, 86:687–705.

Burge, H. A., "Health Effects of Biological Contaminants" (eds. Gammage, R. B., and Berven, B. A.) *Indoor Air and Human Health* (1996), CRC Publishers, Boca Raton.

Burge, H. A., "Indoor Air and Infectious Disease" (eds. Cone, J., and Hodgson, M.), *Problem Buildings:Building-Associated Illness and the Sick Building Syndrome*

(1989), Hanley and Belfus, Philadelphia.

CDC (1999), "Legionellosis: Legionnaire's Disease and Pontiac Fever," Centers for Disease Control, Division of Bacterial and Mycotic Disease, Atlanta.

Clayman, C. B. (ed.), *The American Medical Association Encyclopedia of Medicine* (1989), Random House, New York.

Coggins, C. R., "Growth Characteristics in a Building." In: Jennings, D. H., and Bravery, A. F. (eds.), *Fundamental Biology and Control Strategies* (1991), John Wiley and Sons, East Kilbride, Great Britain.

Finnegan, M. J., and Pickering, C. A. (1984), "Occupational Asthma and Humidifier Fever in Air-Conditioned Buildings," *Proceedings of the Third International Conference of Indoor Air Quality and Climate*, Stockholm.

Flannigan, B., and Morey, P. R., *Control of Moisture Problems Affecting Biological Indoor Air Quality* (1996), ISIAQ, Ottawa.

Foards, K. K., VanOsdell, D. W., and Chang, J. (1996), "Evaluation of Fungal Growth on Fiberglass Duct Materials for Various Moisture, Soil, Use, and Temperature Conditions," *Indoor Air*, 6(2):83–92.

Gammage, R. B., Hansen, D. L., and Johnson, L. W. (1989), "Indoor Air Quality Investigations: A Practitioner's Approach," *Environment International*, 15:503–510.

Garbe, P. L., Davis, B. J., Wesfield, J. S., Markowitz, L. E., Miner, P., Garrity, F., Barbaree, J. M., and Reingold, A. L. (1985), "Nosocomial Legionnaire's Epidemiological Demonstration of Cooling Towers as a Source," *JAMA*, 254:521–524.

Godish, T., *Sick Buildings* (1995), CRC Press, Boca Raton.

Janko, M., Gould, D. C., Vance, L., Stengel, C. C., and Flack, J. (1995), "Dust Mites in Office Environments," *JAMA*, Vol. 56, No. 11, 1133–1140.

Miller, J. D. (1992), "Fungi as Contaminants in Indoor Air," *Atmospheric Environment*, 26a:2163–72.

Milton, D. K., "Bacterial Endotoxins: A Review of Health Effects and Potential Impact in the Indoor Environment" (eds. Gammage, R. B., and Berven, B. A.) *Indoor Air and Human Health* (1996), CRC Publishers, Boca Raton.

Nevalainen, A., "Microbial Contamination of Buildings," *Proceedings of Indoor Air'93*, Helsinki, International Conference on Indoor Air Quality and Climate, Vol. 4, 3–11.

Pasanen, P., Pasanen, A., and Jantunen, M. (1993), "Water Condensation Promotes Fungal Growth in Ventilation Ducts," *Indoor Air,* 3(2):106–112.

Rose, C., "Building-Related Hypersensitivity Diseases: Sentinel Event Management and Evaluation of Building Occupants" (eds. Gammage, R. B., and Berven, B. A.), *Indoor Air and Human Health* (1996), CRC Publishers, Boca Raton.

Rylander, R. (1992), "A Perspective on Indoor Air Microbiological Contamination," *ASHRAE Transactions*, ASHRAE, Atlanta.

Woodard, E. D., Friedlander, B., and Lesher, R. J (1988), "Outbreak of Hypersensitivity Pneumonitis in an Industrial Setting," *JAMA*, 259:1965–1969.

SUGGESTED READINGS

ACGIH Committee on Bioaerosols, *Guidelines for the Assessment of Bioaerosols in the Indoor Environment* (1998), ACGIH, Cincinnati.

Cone, J., and Hodgson, M. (eds.), *Problem Buildings: Building Associated Illness and the Sick Building Syndrome, Occupational Medicine: State of the Art Reviews* (1989), Hanley and Belfus, Philadelphia, 4 (4).

Dillon, H. K., Heinsohn, P. A., and Miller, J. D., *Field Guide for the Determination of Biological Contaminants in Environmental Samples* (1996), AIHA Publications, Fairfax, VA.

Gammage, R., and Berven, B. (eds), *Indoor Air and Human Health* (1996), Lewis Publishers, Boca Raton.

Garbe, P. L., Davis, B. J., and Weisfeld, L. E. (1985), "Nosocomial Legionnaires' disease, epidemiological demonstration of cooling towers as a source," *JAMA*, 254:521–524.

Godish, T., *Sick Buildings* (1995), CRC Press, Boca Raton.

Flannigan, B., and Morey, P. R. *Control of Moisture Problems Affecting Biological Indoor Air Quality* (1996), ISIAQ, Ottawa.

Indoor Air '96, Seventh International Conference on Indoor Air Quality and Climate, Japan.

Chapter 6

Impact of Psychosocial and Other Factors

OVERVIEW

The preceding chapters have concentrated on the pollutants found in the indoor environment and their impact on the health of the occupant.

However, when focusing on building-related environmental complaints including SBS-like symptoms, the causes are considered to be multifaceted in origin, and problems with the physical building environment is only one factor that influences building occupants' well-being. Practitioners have observed that numerous personal, psychological, social, and organizational factors also play important roles. This chapter focuses on the many risk factors including psychosocial and personal characteristics (atopy, female gender, etc.) that impact on occupants' sense of well-being.

INTRODUCTION

The previous chapters have examined various facets of the physical environment that impact on occupants' health. Observations and/or measurements of the physical environment can be used as a guide for gaining insight into such problem areas. There are, however, other, nonmeasurable factors that can impact on a person's sense of well-being, and such factors are particularly significant in cases of building-related environmental complaints, including SBS.

These other factors are most often labeled "psychosocial." There is no standard definition of the psychosocial work environment (Eriksson 1996). However, research to date has focused on the following factors: psychological demands of work (e.g., amount of work, task variety, skill usage); work control (e.g., organizational issues that affect the control workers have); personal development (e.g., new skills); and social support (e.g., support from supervisors and co-workers) (Eriksson 1996). Another way of defining "psychosocial" would be that it covers an individual's interaction with their work/social environment (Markwell 1997).

Most health practitioners believe that there is an intimate relationship between psychosocial and biological processes, and that it is inappropriate to separate the two (Baker 1989). While most (if not all) health practitioners would agree that there is a relationship between health and various psychosocial factors, the nature of that relationship and of the specific psychosocial factors involved is subject to considerable uncertainty. Different researchers, for example, use different definitions of such terms as psychosocial or stress, or they may focus only on one factor, ignoring all others. Furthermore, there is a wide range of opinion on the exact role that psychosocial factors play in building-related illnesses.

When the concept of SBS was in its infancy, it was proposed that SBS was a "mass-psychogenic illness" (MPI). MPI has been defined as "the collective occurrence of physical symptoms and related beliefs among two or more persons in the absence of an identifiable pathogen" (Colligan 1979). However, the symptoms of MPI and SBS proved to be totally different. Unlike SBS, MPI is characterized by the sudden onset of a symptom (such as fainting) and comes to a distinct end; there is little evidence to consider SBS a form of psychogenic illness (Hedge 1989).

One caution must be raised when addressing the impact of psychosocial factors. There is a difference between considering the role of psychosocial factors and "blaming the victim." In other words, the practitioner must not fall into the error of assuming that because psychosocial factors may play a role in SBS, such health problems are "all in a person's head." The cause of SBS seems to be multifaceted; some of the factors most consistently associated with SBS symptoms are (1) building-related, such as air conditioning, carpets, ventilation rates; (2) psychosocial, such as job stress/dissatisfaction; and (3) personal characteristics, more often than not, a person will have a predisposition to allergies (Mendell 1993). It is important to understand that all three factors are probably involved in evoking the complainant's symptoms.

Both psychosocial and environmental factors seem to work in concert and perhaps synergistically in SBS problems. Baker states that "psychological, social, and organizational factors may function both as causative factors in office-building-associated health complaints and as modifiers of the effects of other environmental factors" (Baker 1989).

The diversity of factors that contribute to SBS is exemplified by a study of 4000 EPA employees concerning health symptoms, workplace conditions, and perceived air quality (Wallace 1993). On questionnaires, the employees reported 32 health symptoms that were grouped into 12 health categories. Factors associated with more than 3 "health issues" included (1) workplace characteristics, such as dust and glare; (2) personal characteristics, such as sensitivity to chemical fumes and mold allergies; and (3) psychosocial factors, such as heavy workload and conflicting job demands.

OCCUPATIONAL STRESS

Most health practitioners believe that stress plays an important role in an individual's health. More than a decade ago, Kasl reviewed existing research on stress and disease and defined stress as "demands that tax the adaptive process" (Kasl 1984). This chapter looks at both the external and "internal" demands that can tax an occupant and play a part in SBS.

Kasl suggests that when the objective and subjective (perceived) measures do not correlate that (1) we have not identified properly the actual environmental exposure, (2) the perceived measure has its linkages to a personal characteristic rather than environmental exposure; or (3) the presence of disease has biased the subjective measure (Kasl 1984). All these possibilities may apply in SBS situations.

Most research on occupational stress has focused on the work task itself (Baker 1989). However, any event or condition that places a demand on the individual may result in what is essentially an environmental stress. Such environmental stressors include the physical environment, job structure, work task, organization factors, and extra-organizational factors (Baker 1989).

Baker has designated three components of occupational stress—(1) stressors, (2) outcomes, and (3) modifiers (Baker 1989). The stressors include job structure, such as overtime or shiftwork; task overload and lack of control; physical conditions, such as biological, chemical, or physical hazards; organizational factors, such as role ambiguity and lack of respect; and extra-organizational factors, such as job insecurity and career development.

The outcomes include physiological factors, such as changes in blood pressure; psychological factors, such as anxiety and job dissatisfaction; and behavioral factors, exemplified by absenteeism and reduced productivity.

The modifiers include the individual, such as behavioral style and personal resources, and social support, either emotional or informational. In other words, the personality of the individual and the characteristics of the environment can influence the response to the stress. Whatever the occupational stress, individuals vary greatly in their response, just as individuals vary in their response to an allergen.

Studies have shown that people working in an organization that is reorganizing have increased levels of SBS, perhaps due to worrying about losing their job. Role conflict and workload can have a significant effect on the risk of developing symptoms of SBS (Hedge 1988).

Psychosocial factors such as work load, role conflict, work control, and job satisfaction have been shown to play a significant role when SBS symptoms are reported (Eriksson 1996).

Research indicates that "clerical workers whose jobs are low in technological complexity, mental effort, or contact with the public are more likely to demonstrate higher levels of physiological and psychological stress and strain resulting in impaired health and well-being" (Cohen 1984).

Another major cause of stress is that workers feel vulnerable and unsafe in their office environment since there are numerous illnesses associated with the office environment (cancer caused by exposure to asbestos, pneumonia from exposure to *Legionella* bacteria, etc.). The list of stress-triggering possibilities is long: workers see powdery dust after a renovation and worry about asbestos; they smell a "funny" odor and worry about dangerous gases; they read about lead in drinking water and worry about their drinking fountains, and so on.

The very process of dealing with complaints about the environment may also produce stress. When occupants complain about a workplace, the physical environment is usually evaluated to find a cause. If nothing environmentally suspect is discovered, occupants are told that their environment is acceptable; there may even be insinuations that the problem is psychological in nature and "not based in reality." Office workers may then worry that their workplace has not been adequately evaluated and that some unknown or undiscovered danger exists. In addition to mistrusting their employers (who are prone to blame employees rather than the environment), employees may also mistrust the investigators, who are in effect working for management. The combination of factors—mistrust of management and investigators saying the environment is safe coupled with an excessive workload in an organization that does not appreciate them—can and will cause additional stress and problems.

PERSONAL CHARACTERISTICS

In addition to stress, numerous personal characteristics have been identified as contributing to SBS. These include atopic status, gender, age, marital status, and lifestyle factors such as smoking, alcohol consumption, and regular exercise (Godish 1996). The major risk factors have been identified as atopic history and gender.

Atopic individuals have a tendency to suffer from one or more allergic disorders, such as asthma, eczema, and allergic rhinitis (Clayman 1989). This risk factor, one of the most important for all building-associated illnesses, is discussed in Chapters 2 and 5.

Gender also seems to be a major risk characteristic, with females consistently reporting higher rates of SBS symptoms than males. There are numerous possible explanations for differences in reporting rates. Men may underreport symptoms where there is no obvious environmental cause, since they are less willing to admit "weakness" (Raw 1993). However, when there is an obvious environmental cause, men will report as many symptoms as women.

The gender difference may be influenced by other factors. For instance, women may be subject to different psychosocial and environmental conditions. They may, for example, (1) hold lower positions in the office, which can lead to numerous stresses; (2) work for an extended time with VDTs, which have been shown to be a major SBS risk factor; and (3) work more frequently with paper and office equipment, which have been established as major risk factors (Godish 1996).

It is of interest to note that the gender difference in reporting of SBS symptoms disappears at the highest level of control for all job types (Raw 1993). Numerous factors may come into play; these women's physical working environment may be significantly changed, but they now may also face the same pressures men face not to admit to a "weakness."

SUMMARY

Most health practitioners believe that there is an intimate relationship between psychosocial and biological processes, and that it is inappropriate to separate the two.

Although it is usually difficult to identify a specific cause of SBS, it is probably multifaceted, involving environmental issues plus one or more risk factors; these include atopy, female gender, low job category, problematic psychosocial factors, paper use, VDT work, and mechanical ventilation systems. Psychosocial and biological factors may work in concert and perhaps synergistically in SBS-related problems.

SUGGESTIONS FOR EVALUATION

- Define stress and discuss its role as a factor in SBS-related issues.
- List and discuss the other major psychosocial factors that may play a role in SBS.
- Discuss the personal characteristics that are significant factors in SBS.

KEY WORDS AND CONCEPTS

SBS, atopy, gender, mass-psychogenic illness, psychosocial, stress, allergy, organization, workload, worker control

REFERENCES

Baker, D. B., "Social and Organizational Factors in Office Building-Associated Illness," Cone, J. E., and Hodgson, M. J. (eds.), *Problem Buildings: Building-Associated Illness and the Sick Building Syndrome* (1989), Hanley and Belfus, Philadelphia.

Clayman, C. B. (ed.), *Encyclopedia of Medicine* (1989), Random House, New York.

Cohen, B. G. F., (ed.,) *Human Aspects in Office Automation* (1984), Elsevier, New York.

Colligan, M. J., and Murphy, L. R. (1979), "Mass Psychogenic Illness in Organizations: An Overview," *J. Occupational Psychology*, 52:77–90.

Eriksson, N., Hoog, J., Stenberg, B., and Sundell, J. (1996), "Psychosocial Factors and the Sick Building Syndrome," *Indoor Air*, 2:101–111.

Godish, T., *Sick Buildings* (1996), CRC Press, Boca Raton.

Hedge, A. (1988), "Job stress, job satisfaction, and work-related illness in offices," *Proceeding of the 32nd Annual Meeting, Human Factors Society*, Human Factors Society, Santa Monica, CA.

Hedge, A., Burge, P. S., Robertson, A. S., Wilson, S., and Harris-Bass, J. (1989), "Work-related illness in offices: A proposed model of the SBS," *Environmental International*, 15:143–158

Kasl, S. V. (1984), "Stress and Health," *Ann. Rev. Public Health*, 5:319–341.

Markwell, N., Personal Communication (1997), Union Institute, Cincinnati.

Mendell, M. J. (1993), "Non-specific Symptoms in Office Workers: A Review and

Summary of the Epidemiological Literature," *Indoor Air*, 3:227–236.

Raw, G. J., and Grey, A., "Sex Differences in Sick Building Syndrome," *Indoor Air '93*, Helsinki, Vol. 1, 381–387.

Stenberg, B., Mild, K. H., Sandstrom, M., Sundell, J., and Wall, S. (1993), "A Prevalence Study of the Sick Building Syndrome and Facial Skin Symptoms in Office Workers," *Indoor Air*, 3:71–82.

Wallace, L. A., Nelson, C. J., Highsmith, R., and Dunteman, R. (1993), "Association of Personal and Workplace Characteristics with Health, Comfort and Odor: A Survey of 3948 Office Workers in Three Buildings," *Indoor Air,* 3:193–205.

SUGGESTED READINGS

Baker, D. B., "Social and Organizational Factors in Office Building-Associated Illness," Cone, J. E., and Hodgson, M. J. (eds.), *Problem Buildings: Building-Associated Illness and the Sick Building Syndrome* (1989), Hanley and Belfus, Philadelphia.

Cohen, B. G. F. (ed.), *Human Aspects in Office Automation* (1984), Elsevier, New York.

Godish, T., *Sick Buildings* (1996), CRC Press, Boca Raton.

Kasl, S. V. (1984), "Stress and Health," *Ann. Rev. Public Health* 5:319–341.

Lahtinen, M., and Huuhtanen, P. (1998), "Sick Building Syndrome and Psychosocial Factors—a Literature Review," *Indoor Air*, Supplement 5.

Eriksson, N., Hoog, J., Stenberg, B., and Sundell, J. (1996), "Psychosocial Factors and the Sick Building Syndrome," *Indoor Air,* 6:101–111.

CHAPTER 7

DIAGNOSING IAQ PROBLEMS

OVERVIEW

Health in the nonindustrial workplace is defined as physical, mental, and social well-being, rather than simply the absence of disease, as is the case in the industrial workplace. Therefore, when responding to an IAQ complaint, the practitioner must be cognizant not only of environmental contamination, which is typically so low as to defy interpretation with industrial standards, but also of all other environmental factors (such as temperature) in addition to the psychosocial factors discussed in Chapter 6.

This chapter discusses methods to assist the practitioner in conducting an IAQ investigation. A two-phased investigative approach is generally considered advisable. The first phase consists of interviewing the complainant, reviewing readily available information, and conducting a limited visual inspection of the HVAC system and the problem area. A second phase is initiated when more information is deemed necessary and detailed observations, including measurements, are required. This chapter provides an overview of common measurement techniques and discusses the problems encountered when there are no numerical standards for evaluating results.

LEARNING OUTCOMES

- A knowledge of IAQ evaluation techniques and how they differ from industrial hygiene investigations
- A basic understanding of the differences between phase I and phase II evaluations
- A basic understanding of how to take VOC and microbial measurements, and some of the problems associated with interpreting the results

BACKGROUND

Industrial Hygiene Investigations versus IAQ Investigations

The industrial indoor environment has long been known to be associated with clinically evident adverse health effects. Causal associations between toxic occupational exposures and diseases of many organ systems have been established (Landrigan 1991).

An investigative industrial hygiene (IH) survey involves the evaluation of all exposures to potentially harmful situations and the development of control measures (Clayton 1978). In an IH study, the appropriate measurements are taken and the results are compared to established health standards that provide a reasonable degree of protection for healthy adult workers. Whether or not a workplace is acceptable is dictated totally by measurement; protocols for both sampling and analytical techniques exist and the results can be compared to a standard.

In the industrial workplace, health is defined as the absence of disease. In contrast to this limited definition, health in the nonindustrial sector is defined as physical, mental, and social well-being.

Given such a broad definition, the practitioner must deal with a wide range of issues. Furthermore, an extremely wide variety of circumstances can lead to indoor discomfort, specific information on levels of complex chemical mixtures or biomatter that can cause discomfort or illness is lacking, and people vary greatly in their response to all the factors involved.

In the past, there were attempts to adapt IH standards and techniques, such as using a fraction of the OSHA permissible exposure levels (PEL) as a guide to IAQ acceptability. In fact, ASHRAE Standard 62-89 suggested a tenth of the occupational standard for organic compounds as an IAQ guideline for indoor nonindustrial exposures, but this does not appear in the revised 62-89R draft document. In any case, this guideline was not particularly useful, because a PEL is intended to provide a healthy worker with protection against the individual compounds that tend to dominate in an industrial environment. IAQ guidelines would have to protect individuals who are exposed to low levels of complex mixtures of organic compounds along with other environmental factors that PELs were never intended to address (Gammage 1995).

One of the most daunting but salient factors when responding to an IAQ complaint is that few studies to date have been able to show direct causality between the low levels of contaminants typically found and the symptoms observed. In other words, it is clear that symptoms are present, but how they are related to the workplace is not clear. Because well-being is involved, practitioners cannot just measure contaminants as in an IH investigation; they must be knowledgeable about environmental conditions, relevant personal characteristics, and psychosocial factors as well.

For example, some of the factors most consistently found associated with SBS symptoms can be somewhat loosely characterized as (1) building-related, such as air conditioning, carpets, and ventilation rates; (2) psychosocial, such as job stress/dissatisfaction; and (3) personal characteristics such as allergies/asthma (Mendell 1993). The key difficulty an IAQ practitioner has when responding to a complaint is that all three factors are probably involved somehow in evoking the complainant's symptoms.

IAQ PROTOCOLS

OSHA has estimated that 30 to 70 million American workers are affected by nonoccupational building-related environmental problems (BNA 1992). These large numbers have resulted in the growth of companies conducting IAQ investigations. Most companies have developed their own protocols for diagnosing IAQ problems, incorporating their expertise and in-house analytical skills. For instance, if a company specializes in analytical capabilities, the chances are that testing will be a significant part of its procedures.

Protocols have also been developed by agencies of various countries and health organizations such as the AIHA. Two of the more widely used protocols are "Building Air Quality: A Guide for Building Owners and Facility Managers" by the EPA/NIOSH, and "General Protocol for the Investigation of IAQ Complaints" from ISIAQ. Godish gives an overview of the more prominent protocols (Godish 1995).

The objective of all protocols is to identify the cause of occupant complaints, eliminate the source of the complaint, prevent it from recurring, and avoid creating other problems. In general, most protocols include the following guidelines:

- Interview the concerned party (a written questionnaire is helpful), looking for timing patterns in the occurrence of symptoms. This information can indicate potential causes and provide direction for the investigation.
- Survey the complainant's environment for contaminant sources and pathways.
- Examine and evaluate the status of the HVAC system.
- Formulate a hypothesis (cause and effect) about the cause of the problem.
- Develop and implement an action plan to eliminate the cause (hypothesis testing).
- Discuss the results of the action plan with the complainant.
- Inform the complainant of the progress made to see if the symptoms have been alleviated.
- Conduct a follow-up inspection after a short period of time (perhaps a month).

These steps above usually constitute the first phase of a two-phased approach; they are discussed in more detail below. If these steps solve the problem, no further action is needed.

If more information is needed, the investigation moves to a second phase that includes detailed observations and measurements (see phase II, page 69).

SOLVING IAQ PROBLEMS–PHASE I

Reason for Concern/Scope of Problem

An IAQ survey is usually conducted because of a complaint or complaints. When building occupants complain about poor IAQ, identifying the cause is difficult: (1) symptoms are usually nonspecific and difficult to attribute to one cause; (2) building conditions constantly vary; and (3) reactions between individuals differ based on their sensitivity (Sundell 1996).

The first task is to define the scope of the problem—how many people are complaining and what are they complaining about? This can be accomplished by interviewing the complainant(s), using a questionnaire.

It is very important to find out if the complainant is suffering "subjective" symptoms that usually subside after leaving the building (SBS) or a clinical condition with clinically defined symptoms (e.g., fever, infection) that do not improve after leaving the building (BRI). As discussed in Chapter 2, most building-associated illness is SBS and not BRI. In any case, it is very important to suggest that the complainant get medical advice if the symptoms do not disappear after the person leaves the building.

A questionnaire can be helpful because it will help clarify whether the problem is SBS- or BRI-related, show trends (especially temporal patterns) and also make sure that everyone is asked the same questions, giving the interview process some formal structure. Giving the questionnaire to only the complainants (instead of to a larger group such as the whole floor or building) is not considered statistically valid, but it is advantageous in that those involved can be polled in a short period of time. Building managers often fear that questionnaires will prove upsetting, but most people find the process reassuring, since they feel they are being attended to and that their well-being is important.

A questionnaire should address: (1) the nature of the concern, (2) when the problem is worst and if it lessens or disappears when the complainant leaves the building, (3) whether the complainant has noticed any building conditions that might explain the problem, and (4) if the complainant has experienced any discomfort that might be attributed to other factors such as stress, noisy surroundings, or poor lighting. A sample questionnaire appears as Appendix A of this book.

Initial Walk-through

An initial walk-through of the problem area should provide information about (1) the HVAC system, (2) contaminant sources, (3) pollutant pathways, and (4) the building occupants' activities. The walk-through is best conducted by in-house staff—a building manager or building engineer—since no one better understands how the building operates. If the walk-through is done by an outside consultant, it is important that the building engineer lend support and knowledge.

When conducting the walk-through, keep in mind the factors that are most consistently associated with SBS: temperature, air conditioning, carpets, crowded conditions, VDT use, ventilation rates, job stress/dissatisfaction, and allergies/asthma (Mendell 1993). Note that temperature is the first factor to be considered. A substantial amount of research shows that the thermal environment profoundly influences people's responses, whether they be about health, comfort, satisfaction, or productivity. Temperatures in excess of 75 degrees F will nearly always increase dissatisfaction with IAQ.

HVAC System Screening

In phase I, HVAC systems are given a quick screening to identify factors that might contribute to the problem. It is important to be sure that the components of the HVAC system are functioning properly and that the HVAC system is adequate for the current use of the building. For example, have there been changes in building layout and use since the original design and construction? Has there been increased population in a space without consideration for ventilation needs? Are there signs of occupant discomfort, for instance, small fans located on desks or blocked diffusers because occupants find the space too hot, too cold, or too drafty?

The timing of when the problem occurs and the operation of the HVAC system may be significant. What time does the HVAC system start operating in the morning and when do the occupants start work? Are there problematic processes that operate when the HVAC system is off, such as after office hours?

Contaminant Sources Evaluated

There is a multitude of potential sources of emissions or contamination. Contaminants can originate outside a building—perhaps there is construction work that produces emissions in close proximity to a fresh air intake. There are also countless sources within any building. Contaminants can come from within the HVAC system itself, from building materials, especially if there are ongoing renovations nearby, from occupants' activities (photocopying, printing, etc.), and from operation and maintenance procedures. Any or all of these conditions might cause an IAQ problem.

The interviews and questionnaire should ask about possible new sources of contaminants, particularly any renovations or changes in building use that happened at the same time the problems began. Very few sources of contaminants are continuous; most vary in strength over time, and the investigator might not notice the contaminant because of this.

Pollution Pathways

Information about pollution pathways should also be collected. Architectural and mechanical pathways may allow pollutants to enter the complaint area from surrounding spaces, including the outdoors. Typical pathways include doors, operable windows, stairways, elevator shafts, utility chases, ductwork, and plenums.

Look for pathways that could link emissions from identified sources to the problem area. For example, a building may have a small printing operation that operates intermittently. The VOCs from the printing operation may be transported to another floor via a stairwell, resulting in an intermittent odor that causes stress and concern about health.

Develop and Test Hypothesis

Hypothesis development is a process of identifying and narrowing down possible causes of a problem and proposing a solution (EPA/NIOSH 1991). Pay close attention to the information collected and what solutions are suggested. The "best guess" should be tested by making the appropriate changes that might alleviate the problem. Frequently, a small change is all that is necessary. For example, perhaps a new carpet was put down in the problem areas and the off-gasing of VOCs from the adhesive causes odor problems because the HVAC system is shut down during off hours. Keeping the HVAC system working for an extended time might suffice to reduce the odor issue.

Sometimes a situation is more complex. Consider this example. Workers recently relocated to a newly renovated space say they are not feeling well. Construction materials or new furnishings may be off-gassing VOCs that produce an odor, but other factors may also be at work. Psychosocial issues may play a part because the occupants were moved from an area they liked to a new space where they are not comfortable; even though an investigator might feel that this makes no sense since the new area is so much nicer, that's not the issue. Perhaps the area gets too hot from afternoon sun. Occupants, in addition to being unhappy, may be frightened by the odor and uncomfortable because of high temperatures. If all these factors are not considered, the problems will continue.

At the outset of an investigation, all plausible causes, both IAQ and non-IAQ, should be considered (Sundell 1996). Some of the unrelated causes that can contribute to perceived IAQ problems are thermal discomfort, lighting, noise, ergonomic issues, and nuisance conditions such as odor or dust. One or more of the psychosocial factors outlined in Chapter 6 may also play a role. Few studies have shown direct causality between one factor and SBS; complaints may be caused by a host of factors that individually would not cause a problem, but together do. Common sense can play an important role in conducting these types of investigations.

At the same time, it is important to stay humble, to remember that an investigator's perspective is always greatly influenced by both the climate of the times and what is known at any given moment. One's perspective, for example, may be influenced by the "panic of the moment"—one year, it is asbestos in the air, another year lead in drinking water. What is thought to be "scientific fact" today may be considered nonsense tomorrow. In a review of a book on hysteria, Carol Travis points out: "Until the bacillus that causes tuberculosis was identified, TB was thought to be a result of having a 'tubercular personality.' Until the bacterium that causes peptic ulcers was identified, ulcers were said to be caused by repressed anger—still a favorite psychoanalytic culprit. In California, a woman spent 12 years in therapy, her muscles getting steadily weaker. . . . The psychiatrist said her problem was her 'repressed rage' at her parents; she turned out to have myasthenia gravis, a progressive muscular disease" (Travis 1997). Travis goes on to note: "In the absence of medical certainty, the belief that all . . . symptoms are psychological in origin is no improvement over the belief that none of them are" (Travis 1997). Practitioners are required to tread a sometimes fine line between the extremes, and these issues should be kept in mind when proposing hypotheses as well as when deciding on solutions.

Any efforts to correct an IAQ problem should address their impact on surrounding areas; future problems may be created in other areas by the steps taken to eliminate the problems.

It is important to include follow-up procedures that ensure that the problem has in fact been resolved. This can be accomplished by revisiting the site and interviewing complainants after a period of perhaps two weeks. Sometimes problems disappear only to reappear after time. If all the issues were not addressed or if a timing pattern causes a problem to occur intermittently, further work may be necessary.

SOLVING IAQ PROBLEMS–PHASE II

Sampling Strategy

Sometimes the steps outlined in phase I do not solve the problem. Additional information may be necessary, especially if there is a potential source of a major risk factor such as microbial contamination due to flooding or if data are needed to support a hypothesis.

Whatever the situation, it is important that the sampling and analytical protocol and strategy used will in fact answer the questions asked. Since there is no consensus on nonindustrial exposures to contaminants, prior to conducting measurements a protocol for interpreting the data must be developed. One of the most germane questions is whether the data be interpreted so that it either supports or doesn't support the hypothesis. The following questions should also be addressed with respect to the hypotheses: why measure? what to measure? how to measure? when to measure? where to measure? how often and long to measure? what sampling and analytical method to use so that the results provide useful data?

Potential uses of indoor air measurements include: (1) comparing different areas of the building (e.g., complaint versus noncomplaint), (2) comparing indoor to outdoor conditions, (3) comparing conditions before and after building changes, (4) testing a hypothesis about the source of the problem, and (5) comparing measurements to predetermined guidelines (Rafferty 1993).

HVAC Evaluations

Although phase I includes a quick screening of the HVAC system, phase II entails a more detailed approach to determine whether both ventilation and thermal requirements are being met. The goal is to determine whether the HVAC system is adequate for current use and is functioning properly. Phase II includes an extensive review of all existing documentation, including specifications, any changes from the original design, and current testing and balancing reports. In addition, measurements are taken to confirm that the HVAC system is functioning properly. In some cases, the system may never have operated according to specifications. If the system was never "commissioned" (a process that verifies that everything functions according to specifications), this might be the case.

ISIAQ's quantitative HVAC protocol includes measuring temperature, relative humidity, and carbon dioxide for several days; conducting an engineering analysis; and conducting a detailed air balancing. Testing and balancing involves the testing, adjusting, and balancing of HVAC components so that the entire system provides airflows that are in accordance with the design specifications. Typical components and system parameters tested include all supply, return, exhaust, and outdoor airflow rates, control settings, air temperatures, fan speeds, and filter resistance.

ISIAQ's protocol also includes tracing ventilation pathways using a tracer gas, such as sulfur hexafluoride (SF_6). There are two types of tracer gas techniques—the "step-up" approach and the "decay" approach. The step-up approach involves injecting a tracer gas at a constant rate into the building supply airstream and monitoring the tracer gas concentration in areas of concern and in the exhaust. The decay approach starts with a uniform tracer gas concentration in the areas of concern and then monitors the decay of the concentration in the problem area and the return or exhaust. The performance of the HVAC system pursuant to how much fresh air is being introduced and the distribution patterns can be ascertained by using one of these methods (Breum 1993). However, such tests are a technically demanding and must be done by experienced professionals.

Part of this HVAC evaluation is an extensive and thorough visual inspection to see whether the HVAC system itself may be a source of contaminants. Look for deterioration (corrosion) or conditions such as water damage or standing water that can lead to microbial growth. Check for visible fungal growth or moldy odors, poorly maintained filters, and any staining or discoloration of materials such as ceiling tiles. If the mechanical room serves as a mixing plenum (i.e., return and outdoor air), check for deteriorated insulation and stored chemicals. (Mixing chambers are a favorite place for storing maintenance materials.)

In order to accomplish this type of inspection, it is imperative to look inside the system. If there are no access panels that permit a visual examination, they will have to be cut in the appropriate places.

VOC Evaluation

If volatile organic compounds are of concern, there are two basic sampling methods—on-site collection/measurement or on-site collection with subsequent laboratory analysis. On-site measurement usually entails direct reading survey instruments, employing measurement techniques such as portable flame ionization (FID), photoionization (PID), or infrared spectrophotometry. These techniques lack overall sensitivity and specificity for IAQ studies, but they can be used for screening VOCs, since a lot of measurements can be taken and the results are immediate.

The sampling methods used in conjunction with laboratory analysis are (1) a passive technique such as diffusion or (2) active flow created by airpumps. Passive sampling was developed for the industrial environment; its main disadvantages are that it requires long sampling periods and that environmental variables such as velocity, humidity, and temperature can influence results.

One of the most common active flow techniques is a dynamic sampling system (air pump) with multisorbent tubes. VOCs are collected and concentrated on a solid multibed tube by pulling air through the tube using low-flow sampling pumps. The collected VOCs are thermally desorbed, which provides up to a 1000-fold increase in sensitivity.

Another sampling technique utilizes stainless steel canisters—SUMMA (brand name) canisters are popular. An air sample is drawn through a sampling train composed of components that regulate the rate and duration of sampling into a pre-evacuated canister. After the air sample is collected, the VOCs are identified by gas chromatography/mass spectroscopy, following EPA's method IP-IB (Winberry 1993). Gas chromatography/mass spectrometry is the generally preferred method for analysis of unknown VOCs, since the technique employs a computerized library that can identify compounds.

One of the major advantages of the multisorbent tube collection/measurement technique is that it provides an increase by 3 orders of magnitude in sensitivity. Also, the sampling procedure is relatively easy. The advantage of the canister method is it can collect both real-time and integrated samples. On the other hand, canisters are bulky and require a complex cleaning procedure.

No matter what sampling technique is used, identifying VOCs can be problematic due to analytical costs, laboratory turnaround time, and how the data should be interpreted.

Microbial Evaluations

There is no universal sampling technique for all types of bioaerosols, so the sampling technique is dictated by the purpose or reason for sampling. This section lists some basic sampling techniques for bioaerosols; the sources in the suggested reading list provide more specific information.

Air-sampling viable impaction devices is the most widely accepted method for studies of bioaerosols. The basic technique is the same for most impaction devices: a sampling pump forces the air through a collector that houses either a growth medium for recovering viable organisms or a filtration system to collect particles.

There are different types of collection systems; slit impactors, sieve impactors, filter cassettes, centrifugal impactors, and all-glass impingers are some of the techniques used (sieve impactors are the most widely used in microbial studies). In all cases, the results are usually reported as colony-forming units per cubic meter of air (CFU/m^3).

Another technique for assessing airborne biomatter is the use of air-settling plates. Air-settling plates are usually large petri dishes containing a growth medium; they are placed uncovered in an area of interest for a specified period of time. The choice of growth medium dictates what is collected; some culture a specific type of microorganism, while nondifferential growth media permits the recovery of a wide range of organisms. Air-settling plates are not useful in indoor assessment studies because the different particle settling rates and disturbances due to air currents prohibit useful interpretation of data.

In yet another technique, samples of suspected contamination are taken by swabbing surfaces with either a wet sterile cotton wool-tipped stick or with a piece of cheesecloth using a template to help quantify the microbial contamination for the area sampled (Dillon 1996). Swab samples are then wiped on the surface of the chosen agar medium and cultured according to appropriate protocol.

Bulk (dust) samples can be collected by numerous techniques, usually by applying a vacuum to a bag or filter. The microbial contamination from the collected sample is extracted with water, the extract is then serially diluted and placed on the desired agar medium.

The relationship between bulk source of microorganisms and airborne concentration is not known because of factors such as air movement and physical agitation (Reynolds 1996). A building could have significant microbial contamination that is not reflected by airborne microbial concentration. That is why visual examinations are imperative.

However, it may be helpful to do comparative airborne studies (e.g., outdoors versus indoors, variations in occupants' activities, variables with the ventilation system, problem areas versus areas where there are no complaints). In any studies absolute numbers may be misleading. For example, samples in one area may have a predominance of one type of species and another area may have the same total CFU/m^3 but no predominant species. Further visual investigations would be needed to find out why.

SUMMARY

One of the most daunting but significant factors in responding to an IAQ complaint is that only a few SBS studies have been able to show direct causality between low exposures of contaminants typically found and the symptoms observed. Even so, the determinant factors tend to be (1) building-related, such as having mechanical ventilation; (2) psychosocial, such as job stress; and (3) personal characteristics; such as allergies. In all likelihood, all three factors will be involved when complaints occur.

The first step is to determine if the complainant is suffering from SBS symptoms that subside or a clinical condition with defined symptom (BRI). A medical examination may be required, but if the symptoms disappear after leaving the problem area, the chances are the problem is SBS not BRI.

The objective of evaluations is to identify the cause of occupant complaints, eliminate the source of the complaint, and prevent it from recurring without creating other problems. A two-phased approach is the basis of most established protocols, with the first phase consisting of interviews, a review of all readily available information, and a visual inspection of the problem area and the HVAC system. If necessary, this is followed by a second phase, including more specific measurements, keeping in mind that if measurements are taken, it is important to know how they will be interpreted before sampling.

Eliminating the reasons for discomfort is a process that includes developing a hypothesis, implementing the desired changes, and determining if there is an improvement. It is therefore important for the investigator to maintain contact with the people experiencing problems to ensure that their environment has been improved.

SUGGESTIONS FOR EVALUATION

- Compare IAQ investigations to IH investigations.
- Give an overview of phase I and phase II IAQ evaluation.
- Describe the different techniques of taking (a) VOC and (b) microbial measurements.
- Discuss why measurements taken during phase II are so difficult to interpret.

KEY CONCEPTS AND WORDS

SBS, BRI, questionnaires, IAQ protocols, ISIAQ, EPA/NIOSH, phase I, visual evaluation, phase II, VOC measurements, multisorbent tubes, GC/MS, microbial measurements, viable impaction, SUMMA canister, CFU/m^3, HVAC, SF_6, testing and balancing

REFERENCES

BNA, "Occupational Safety and Health Report" (1992), 921097.

Breum, N. O. (1993), "Diagnosis of Ventilation by Single-Tracer Gas Techniques," *Indoor Air*, Supplement 1.

Clayton, G., and Clayton, F. (eds.), *Patty's Industrial Hygiene and Toxicology* (1978), third edition, Vol. 1, Wiley-Interscience, New York.

Dillon, H. K., Heinsohn, P. A., and Miller, J. D. (eds.), *Field Guide for the Determination of Biological Contaminants in Environmental Samples* (1996), AIHA Publications, Fairfax, VA.

EPA/NIOSH, *Building Air Quality: A Guide for Building Owners and Facility Managers* (1991), U.S. Government Printing Office, Washington, DC.

Gammage, R., and Berven, B. (eds.), *Indoor Air and Human Health* (1996), Lewis Publishers, Boca Raton.

Godish, T., *Sick Buildings, Definition, Diagnosis and Mitigation* (1995), CRC Press, Boca Raton.

Landrigan, P., and Baker, D. (1991), "The Recognition and Control of Occupational Disease," *JAMA,* 266(5):676–860.

Mendell, M. (1993), "Non-specific Symptoms in Office Workers: A Review and Summary of the Epidemiologic Literature," *Indoor Air*, Vol. 4.

Rafferty, P. J. (ed.), *The Industrial Hygienist's Guide to Indoor Air Quality Investigations* (1993), AIHA Publications, Fairfax, VA.

Reynolds, S. J., Morey, P. R., and Gifford, S. M. (1996), "Case Study of Factors Contributing to a Crisis Building," *Indoor Air*, 6(3):168–181.

Sundell, J., and Light, E., *General Protocol for the Investigation of IAQ Complaints* (1996), ISIAQ, Inc., Ottawa, Canada.

Travis, C. (1997), "Review on Hystories: A Book by Elaine Showalter," *New York Times Book Review*, May 4.

Winberry, W. T., Forehand, L., Murphy, N. T., Ceroli, A., Phinney, B., and Evans, A., *Methods for Determination of Indoor Air Pollutants* (1993), Noyes Data Corp., Park Ridge, NJ.

SUGGESTED READINGS

Dillon, H. K., Heinsohn, P. A., and Miller, J. D. (eds.), *Field Guide for the Determination of Biological Contaminants in Environmental Samples* (1996), AIHA Publications, Fairfax, VA.

EPA/NIOSH, *Building Air Quality: A Guide for Building Owners and Facility Managers* (1991), U.S. Government Printing Office, Washington, DC.

Godish, T., *Sick Buildings: Definition, Diagnosis and Mitigation* (1995), CRC Press, Boca Raton.

Sundell, J., and Light, E., *General Protocol for the Investigation of IAQ Complaints* (1996), ISIAQ Inc., Ottawa, Canada.

Weekes, D. M., and Gammage, R. B. (eds.), *The Practitioner's Approach to Indoor Air Quality Investigations* (1990), AIHA Publications, Fairfax, VA.

Winberry, W. T., Forehand, L., Murphy, N. T., Ceroli, A., Phinney, B., and Evans, A., *Methods for Determination of Indoor Air Pollutants* (1993), Noyes Data Corp., Park Ridge, NJ.

Wolkoff, P. (1995), "Volatile organic Compounds—Sources, Measurement, Emissions, and the Impact on Indoor Air Quality," *Indoor Air,* Supplement 3.

Chapter 8

PRO-ACTIVE WAYS OF PREVENTING IAQ PROBLEMS

OVERVIEW

Indoor air quality has a significant effect on productivity, absenteeism, and building occupants' general feeling of well-being. A pro-active program designed to reduce the likelihood of problematic exposures and conditions is the most cost-effective approach to maintaining good indoor air quality.

A pro-active approach concentrates on (1) keeping pollution sources at a low level and (2) maintaining hygienic conditions, which depend not only on how a building has been constructed but also on how it is operated and maintained.

An effective plan for maintaining acceptable indoor air quality must focus on the following fundamental elements: communication, prevention of potential problems, maintenance and operations, training and education, and inspections (Gallo 1993). The goal, in each case, is to institute a comprehensive plan that can be implemented and monitored by in-house staff on a regular basis.

LEARNING OUTCOMES

- A basic understanding of how to design and implement a pro-active program
- A knowledge of procedures to improve indoor air quality
- An appreciation for how important these programs are in reducing occupant distress

INTRODUCTION

IAQ consultants, engineers, and researchers believe indoor air quality has a significant effect on productivity, absenteeism, and occupants' feeling of well-being. Research at the Swedish Building Research Institute, for example, has shown productivity can decrease 20, 30, and perhaps as much as 50% due to the symptoms of SBS (Wyon 1991). It is difficult to obtain exact numbers, in part because of the subjective nature of SBS and in part because of the varied work that is conducted in a nonindustrial workplace.

Although indoor environmental quality complaints are often difficult to attribute to a specific causal agent (see Chapter 7), studies have shown that comfort variables such as hot stuffy air and a dusty office are closely associated with reduced productivity on the job. Absenteeism is often associated with dust and mold allergies, sensitivity to chemicals, and psychosocial variables. (Wallace 1993).

Given the difficulty of identifying specific causes of SBS, research suggests that appropriate prevention and mitigation may need to be at the level of prudent design and sound operation and maintenance practices, focused on factors that reduce the likelihood of problematic exposures and conditions (Mendell 1993).

Simple procedures can help eliminate potential sources of problems or even the perception that a building has poor air quality. This can be done by (1) keeping pollution sources at a low level and (2) maintaining hygienic conditions, which depend not only on how a building has been constructed but also on how it is operated and maintained.

Pro-active programs are the most cost-effective way to prevent or reduce problems associated with poor indoor environment, but "hard numbers" about their effectiveness are difficult to come by. Increased productivity, reduced absenteeism, and occupants' improved sense of well-being are not easy to document. Other factors that make pro-active programs worthwhile are similarly hard to chronicle. For instance, once workers perceive their workplace to be unsafe, it is extremely difficult to change this perception; consequently, any pro-active steps taken to improve comfort and reduce the likelihood of problems can be extremely cost-effective.In addition, relatively low-cost pro-active programs can save a company the often enormous costs of dealing with a preventable environmental emergency or crisis.Pro-active programs can also be a way to prevent or reduce the potential for costly litigation.

Pro-active programs are, in spite of their value, the exception rather than the rule in most companies. In addition to the difficulties of "selling" such programs to top management when there are no hard numbers to support their adoption, such programs rarely provide instant gratification or dramatic ongoing benefits (the absence of problems is sometimes the only sign that a program is successful). Moreover, pro-active programs tend to be the first to be dropped if a company is experiencing financial or other difficulties. In today's marketplace, only "enlightened" firms promote pro-active practices and encourage their employees to follow them.

An effective plan for maintaining acceptable indoor air quality must focus on the following fundamental elements: communication, reduction of potential problems, maintenance and operations, training and education, and inspections (Gallo 1993). These elements, which are intertwined, are discussed more fully below. The goal, in each case, is to institute a comprehensive plan that can be implemented and monitored by in-house staff on a regular basis.

There is one other key element in a successful pro-active program, that is the support of top management. Like any total quality management program, pro-active programs are an ongoing process that requires constant encouragement and support from top management.Without the support of top management, pro-active programs are doomed. Management must also reinforce the importance of each individual's role in providing occupants with a comfortable and safe working environment—and encourage the many groups whose work impacts on the indoor environment to cooperate in maintaining a good environment.

ASHRAE Standard 62-89R "Ventilation for Acceptable Indoor Air Quality"—at this time under public review—contains extensive information about pro-active ventilation design criteria, operating and maintaining a building properly, and dealing with ongoing construction activities within an occupied building. Because of the importance of this document, its recommendations are used extensively in this chapter.

COMMUNICATION

Good communication is a crucial part of a pro-active program. This involves regular and detailed communications between management and staff, between different in-house groups, and between building managers, medical support staff, and occupants. It is important to have written communication guidelines in place for emergencies, but it is equally important to build trust by implementing a formal communication plan for routine activities. A good pro-active program includes procedures for occupants experiencing poor IAQ, for facility operators to routinely inform occupants about any building changes that might effect them, and for different departments to work together to ensure a good environment.

For example, significant VOC emissions may be produced when lacquers, paints, and adhesives are applied. Since these emissions can lead to IAQ problems, it is essential to have good communication between the groups involved in planning and implementing the project (contractors and building operations). It is equally important to notify building occupants who may be affected by the application, telling them when the work will take place, what is being done to reduce VOC emissions, and that there might nevertheless be some noticeable odors.

Responsible Person

ASHRAE Draft Standard 62-89R recommended that one person be responsible for implementation of a pro-active program. Although this draft was not passed, some of the proposed guidelines for prevention of problems were beneficial, such as instituting a responsible person. That person oversees the maintenance and operation of the ventilation system, ensuring that in-house inspections are conducted with the goal of creating an environment that is continually improving, not to criticize any shortcomings. The designated person also reviews inspection results and makes sure that any problems are corrected.

The designated person is also responsible for seeing that any IAQ complaints are responded to. The biggest mistake that building managers can make in the face of an IAQ complaint is to underestimate the problems that can result if occupants believe no action is being taken or that important information is being withheld. It is not unusual to hear employees complain that their opinions and suggestions are not valued or that they have not been informed about building managers' efforts to solve problems. The designated person can help prevent such situations. Understanding the importance of good communication is a key facet of a pro-active program.

Risk Communication

Even with a good pro-active program, problems will inevitably occur, and some situations will evoke fear and "outrage" from building occupants and/or neighbors.These potentially volatile situations might be caused by mysterious odors, by asbestos flaking onto desks during a renovation, or by whatever raises alarm.

One of the most difficult issues that facility managers face is "risk communication" in the face of such alarm. Risk communication can involve either calming people down when they are excessively alarmed about a minor hazard or helping them deal with serious hazards (Sandman 1993).

Responding correctly to such situations is a difficult and complex task, one beyond the scope of this book ("Responding to Community Outrage" is highly recommended for its treatment of the topic.) Suffice it to say here that acknowledgement of the problem is the essence of a successful approach. Ignoring a problem will not make it go away and may in fact make matters worse.

Sometimes an alarming situation is not really dangerous, and all that is needed is an explanation of what caused the problem and what (if any) steps have been taken to prevent a recurrence. Conversely, the designated person may need to acknowledge that mistakes have been made or that there is a dangerous situation but steps are being taken to correct it. In some cases, an apology from top management may be necessary. In all cases, it is important to treat any alarming situations promptly, honestly, and respectfully.

PREVENTING POTENTIAL PROBLEMS

Design Criteria

A building design should promote a comfortable environment in which the majority of occupants express no dissatisfaction. This requires (1) supplying enough air to sufficiently reduce bioeffluents and building-related contaminants, (2) maintaining a temperature that is perceived to be acceptable, (3) limiting unwanted moisture and infiltration of unconditioned air into the building, and (4) curtailing the sources of VOCs.

A design that addresses the occupants' environmental needs is the key to achieving these goals. However, a major obstacle to success is that over time there are changes in a building's occupancy and activities. Designers do not usually allow for sufficient flexibility for changes in building use. Incorporating great flexibility in the initial design is usually not realistic because of cost factors, even though subsequent unplanned demands on the space may result in poor air quality.

Often, the best that can be done is to deal with the problems that arise when changes occur. For example, a space may be designed to accommodate 10 people, but because of consolidation, the company relocates another 10 people to the same area. Since the HVAC system was not designed to accommodate 20 people, IAQ problems will occur. The operations people will be asked to correct the situation, but they cannot introduce more fresh air than the system is designed for. If, however, the designers in charge of renovations consult with the operations people and incorporate their input, the chances are the renovation will be a better one.

Construction: Renovation and Remodeling

Renovation and remodeling are routinely conducted in most buildings. These processes must be carefully designed and monitored because they may disturb problematic materials or involve new materials with high emission rates. Furthermore, buildings are usually at least partially occupied during renovations, and the likelihood of complaints is high.

The following procedures are recommended to minimize degradation of the indoor air quality and to protect those performing such activities as well as employees in other areas of the building:

- Isolate work areas during construction or renovation; keep these areas under negative pressure relative to the adjacent spaces.
- Maximize outside air ventilation, preferably with at least 5 air changes per hour of outside air, when installing "wet" products (caulks, adhesives, paints, sealants, etc.).
- Schedule construction or installation of furnishings so that any buildup of high levels of contaminants can disperse before occupants return to the area.
- Install adsorptive surfaces such as textiles, insulations, and carpets after applying "wet" products, whenever possible.
- Maximize ventilation during installation of materials. Seal return-air ducts and use direct exhaust to the outdoors either through operable windows or through temporary openings.
- Install duct insulation on the perimeter of the ducts and not inside, whenever possible, since fleecy materials may become sinks of organic matter that can support the growth of microbial matter.

Source Control

There are many sources of chemical pollution in the indoor environment. A wide variety of substances are emitted by building construction materials and interior furnishings, appliances, equipment, supplies, human activities, and biological agents. Building materials (adhesives, caulking, paints, etc.) and furnishings (carpets, synthetic furniture, etc.) in particular emit a variety of volatile organic compounds (VOCs) that have been linked to indoor air quality problems. The probability of contaminants is related to the age of the material: the newer the material, the higher its potential for emitting contaminants. Fleecy materials such as carpets can also act as a sponge or sink in which VOCs are absorbed and then reemitted later.

The potential for exposure to chemical contamination will vary according to the characteristics of the building. These include its age, types of materials used in its construction, and type of equipment and supplies used by building occupants. The design, maintenance, and operation of the building's HVAC system as well as general housekeeping practices can greatly influence the levels of contaminants that exist.

Source control is a particularly cost-effective approach to mitigating potential IAQ problems. Removing or reducing the source of contamination may be done by:

- Selecting products that produce fewer or less potent contaminants.
- Conditioning products (allowing VOCs to off-gas) before installation.
- Relocating contaminant-producing equipment to a more appropriate space.
- Isolating emitting products through containment or encapsulation.
- Practicing proper housekeeping to reduce chemical spills, buildup of dust and molds, etc.
- Maintaining equipment and furnishings properly.

All the above are prudent steps in reducing contaminants.However, the first step—product selection—is crucial since the emissions from different versions of each product can vary by orders of magnitude. It is recommended that emission rate testing data be required from manufacturers or suppliers of the following types of materials: coatings, floor or wall coverings, furniture or furnishings, office machines, supplies, and maintenance materials. (Most major suppliers have pertinent emission data on their products; if a supplier does not, consider another source.) In addition, materials should be handled, installed, and maintained in a manner that will produce the least harmful effects on the occupants of the building.

OPERATIONS AND MAINTENANCE

A pro-active program is designed to maintain a clean and dry building and to promote the following goals:

- Mechanical equipment and building surfaces are maintained in sanitary conditions.
- Significant emission sources are isolated from occupied space.
- Only low-emission materials are used.
- Operations, maintenance, and construction activities are performed in a manner that minimizes occupant exposure to contaminants.

Most of these issues can be assessed by inspection and regulated by sound work practices and a standardized maintenance and operations program. It is important to design programs and procedures for reducing occupants' potential environmental exposure and to integrate such programs into existing staff routines.

The HVAC system, the heart of a building, plays a crucial role in any pro-active program, since its effective design, operation, and maintenance are critical to an acceptable indoor environment. Adequate filtration is a critical factor in ensuring a clean system; it reduces the need for cleaning and is the principal method for control of dust. It is recommended that in excess of 60% efficiency filters be used whenever possible. Although these filters are expensive, once dirt has entered an HVAC system it is extremely hard to remove, and dirt is a precursor for microbial growth.

HVAC systems provide multiple sites for microbial growth as well as the means to disperse the microbes throughout the ventilated space. Preventive maintenance is probably the single most important factor for controlling microbial growth in HVAC systems and other areas. This includes prevention of the accumulation of dirt and moisture and prompt attention to unusual situations (such as flooding) that could result in bioaerosol problems. A maintenance and operations audit should be conducted by in-house staff on a routine basis (see Inspections on page 82).

Housekeeping Practices

Cleaning is a powerful tool for environmental control since it improves the environmental condition quickly and visibly, reduces human frustration and anxiety, and protects human health (Berry 1994). For example, EPA studies showed that "dust" was the workplace variable that affected the largest number of health symptoms and comfort/odor concerns; dust was also identified as the characteristic that contributed the most to a wide variety of health, comfort, and odor concerns (Wallace 1993). Therefore, a program of routine dusting and cleaning will be extremely beneficial.

As with all the other elements of a pro-active program, good communication, in this instance between maintenance staff and occupants, is important. For instance, dusting in offices occurs only in the areas that are clear of papers, books, etc. Thus, it is helpful to tell people when cleaning will occur and ask that they clear the areas they want cleaned. This type of communication enlists occupants' participation in the process.

Cleaning products themselves can contribute significantly to indoor air pollution. Their composition and usage—how much surface area will be exposed to circulating air and how much of the product is used—are crucial.

Proper application of cleaning chemicals is critical, but workers typically are not educated about the impact of these cleaners in relation to the quality of the indoor environment. It is quite common, for example, to use a more concentrated cleaning solution than recommended, in the misconception that the work will be easier. Such actions can have serious consequences for the environment. A brief and simple training program by the designated person can counteract this problem.

Although material safety data sheets (MSDS) are invaluable when investigating an industrial complex, they have limited value when evaluating most products used in cleaning office complexes. Most offices use commercial cleaning agents containing a myriad of chemicals, which in sufficient airborne concentration can cause poor IAQ. More and more "green" products that substitute natural substances for chemicals are now being produced, and their use is recommended.

TRAINING AND EDUCATION

An ongoing training/education program is an important component of a pro-active program. Otherwise, a program will exist without proper implementation, which is equivalent to having no program at all.

The education of the designated IAQ person is especially important.This person should be knowledgeable about the principles of ventilation system operation and maintenance, and be familiar with ASHRAE standards and the specific ventilation system serving the building. The designated person should also be informed about all other factors that impact on building occupants, including psychosocial factors.

Some formal training in indoor environmental quality issues will probably be advisable for the designated person, who should also keep current with developments in the field. Organizations such as the American Society of Heating Refrigeration Air Conditioning Engineers (ASHRAE) and the International Society of Indoor Air Quality (ISIAQ) regularly hold conferences on indoor air.

Once the responsible person has a good understanding of IAQ issues, he/she can begin to train other staff members in understanding the importance of being pro-active. Regular meetings with housekeeping and maintenance staffs can be helpful. In addition, it is important that management be kept knowledgeable and involved in supporting a pro-active program.

It must be acknowledged that even though staff members should become as knowledgeable as possible, the services of an IAQ advisor/consultant will be quite beneficial. The field of indoor air quality is growing quickly, and a consultant who keeps abreast of the ever-expanding knowledge can be an important component of a program.

INSPECTIONS

Inspections serve to (1) identify potential problems, (2) allow facilities management to take action on any identified concerns, and (3) confirm that the programs are working (Sawers 1993).

A monthly inspection by in-house staff should focus on the HVAC system, concentrating on moisture and dirt. The EPA recommends routine inspection of outdoor air dampers, coiling coils and other parts of the HVAC system as well as maintenance procedures that include changing particulate filters on a regular schedule. An example of an inspection audit that can help facilitate conducting inspections is found in Appendix A; this form can be adapted to accommodate the logistics and particulars of a building.

To augment the in-house inspections, an outside consultant can be utilized to conduct inspections on a more infrequent basis, perhaps on a semiannual basis. The use of an outside consultant ensures that the HVAC system is being maintained properly and reinforces the importance of inspections.

The inspection plan should include any water treatment programs such as microbial control (especially for *Legionella*) in cooling-tower water systems. A testing program should be implemented to verify the effectiveness of the water treatment program, and this program should be monitored by the IAQ personresponsible for the operations and maintenance program.

SUMMARY

Research suggests that a pro-active program can prevent or mitigate potential IAQ problems. An effective plan includes the following fundamental elements: communication, reduction of potential problems, maintenance and operations, training and education, and inspections. The support of top management is also crucial.

A crucial part of a pro-active program is to have good communications—between management and staff, and between different in-house groups, medical support staff, and occupants. It is helpful to designate one individual to be responsible for the program and to have a formalized written program that reinforces a pro-active approach.

Most problems can be prevented or regulated by sound work practices and standardized maintenance and operations programs that can be assessed by in-house inspections. It is important to design programs and procedures for reducing occupants' environmental exposure and to integrate such programs in existing staff routine.

SUGGESTIONS FOR EVALUATION

- What are the essential components of a pro-active program?
- Why is a pro-active program so important?
- What are some of the ways to make sure a pro-active program is implemented?

KEY CONCEPTS AND WORDS

Communication, cleaning practices, design criteria, inspections, productivity, product selection, renovation, responsible person, source control, training and education, operations and maintenance

REFERENCES

ASHRAE Draft Standard 62-89R, "Ventilation for Acceptable Indoor Air Quality: Public Review Draft" (1996), ASHRAE, Atlanta.

Breum, N. O. (1993), "Diagnosis of Ventilation by Single-Tracer Gas Techniques" *Indoor Air*, Supplement 1/93.

EPA/NIOSH, *Building Air Quality: A Guide for Building Owners and Facility Managers* (1991), U.S. Government Printing Office, Washington, DC.

Gallo, F. M. (1993), "Maintaining a Healthy Building," *Proceedings of Indoor Air '93*, Helsinki, 6:313–316.

Tavris, C. (1997), "Pursued by Fashionable Furies," *New York Times Book Review*, May 4, 28–29.

Mendell, M. (1993), "Non-Specific Symptoms in Office Workers: A Review and Summary of the Epidemiologic Literature," *Indoor Air*, 4.

Sandman, P. M., *Responding to Community Outrage* (1993), AIHA Publications, Fairfax, VA.

Sawers, J. (1993), "Pro-Active IAQ Audits," *Proceedings of Indoor Air '93*, Helsinki, 6:343–348.

Sundell, J., and Light, E., *General Protocol for the Investigation of IAQ Complaints* (1996), ISIAQ Inc., Ottawa, Canada.

Wallace, L. A., Nelson, C. J., Highsmith, R., and Dunteman, R. (1993), "Association of Personal and Work-Place Characteristics with Health, Comfort and Odor: A Survey of 3948 OfficeWorkers in Three Buildings," *Indoor Air*, 3:193–205.

Wyon, D. (1991), "The Ergonomics of Healthy Buildings: Overcoming Barriers to Productivity," *IAQ '91*, ASHRAE, Atlanta.

SUGGESTED READING

ASHRAE Draft Standard 62-89R, "Ventilation for Acceptable Indoor Air Quality: Public Review Draft" (1996), ASHRAE, Atlanta.

Berry, M. A., *Protecting the Building Environment: Cleaning for Health* (1994), Tricomm 21st Press, Chapel Hill.

Cone, J. E., and Hodgson, M. J. (eds.), *Problem Buildings: Building Associated Illness and the Sick Building Syndrome* (1989), Halley and Belfus, Philadelphia.

EPA/NIOSH, *Building Air Quality: A Guide for Building Owners and Facility Managers* (1991), U.S. Government Printing Office, Washington, DC.

EPA (1998), "Building Air Quality Action Plan" (EPA Publication #402-K-98-001).

Flannigan, B., and Morey, P. R., *Control of Moisture Problems Affecting Biological Indoor Air Quality* (1996), ISIAQ Inc., Ottawa, Canada.

Godish, T., *Sick Buildings: Definition, Diagnosis and Mitigation* (1995), CRC Press, Boca Raton.

Sandman, P. M., *Responding to Community Outrage* (1993), AIHA Publications, Fairfax, VA.

Sundell, J., and Light, E., *General Protocol for the Investigation of IAQ Complaints* (1996), ISIAQ Inc., Ottawa, Canada.

APPENDIX A

INDOOR AIR QUALITY QUESTIONNAIRE BUILDING OPERATIONS

Building/Location ______________________________

Occupant Name ______________________________

Phone Number ______________________________

Interviewer ______________________________

Date ______________________________

1. What is the nature of the concern? Please be as detailed as possible.

____

____

____

____

____

____

____

2. The problem is worst during

DAY

_____ early morning
_____ late morning
_____ early afternoon
_____ late afternoon
_____ evening

WEEK

_____ Monday
_____ Tuesday
_____ Wednesday
_____ Thursday
_____ Friday
_____ Weekend

When does the problem lessen or disappear?

____
____
____
____
____
____

3. Have you noticed any building conditions that might need attention or might help explain your problem (e.g., temperature, humidity, drafts, stagnant air, odors)

____
____
____
____
____
____

4. Have you noticed any other events (such as change of season, weather, temperature or humidity, or activities in the building) that tend to occur around the same time as your problem?

____
____
____
____
____
____

5. Have you experienced any discomfort that might be attributed to any of the following factors?

_____ inadequate or poor lighting
_____ noisy surroundings
_____ fatigue or other problems associated with the performance of your job
_____ stress
_____ plants or other vegetation
_____ other (please specify)

6. Do you have any other comments/observations?

____
____
____
____
____
____

7. Findings/Recommendations

____
____
____
____
____
____

8. Follow-up interview (scheduled no later than 1 month after initial interview)

____
____
____
____
____
____

APPENDIX B
MONTHLY INSPECTION

This form is used to record information obtained during the inspection of the HVAC system and its major components. Record your fmdings for each floor by indicating Y (yes) or N (no), S (satisfactory) or NS (not satisfactory), or other response as noted below.

Date of Inspection: ________________ Inspector: ________________________

Mechanical room

general condition ____

used for storage ____

System check-out

Supply fan

operating ____

correct direction of fan rotation ______________________________

correct airflow direction ____________________________________

Return fan

operating ____

correct direction of fan rotation ______________________________

correct airflow direction ____________________________________

Exhaust fan

operating ____

correct direction of fan rotation ______________________________

correct airflow direction ____________________________________

Outdoor air intake

indicate open/closed ____________________

Air handler housing

general condition ____________________

sound liner ____________________

Air handler components

general condition intakes ____________________

dampers ____________________

coils ____________________

drain pans ____________________

fan belts ____________________

Air distribution ductwork

general condition ____________________

leakage at seams ____________________

liners ____________________

Exhaust fans

general condition ____________________

fan belts ____________________

Terminal units

general condition ____________________

dampers ____________________

Control system

general condition ____________________

sensors ____________________

Particulate filtration systems

general condition ____________________

accessibility ____________________

filter fit into frames ____________________

filter condition ______________________________

evenness of loading ______________________________

indicator of resistance ______________________________

time to change label ______________________________

pressure indicator reading ______________________________

(Pa or in.) ______________________________

Cooling towers

general condition ______________________________

surfaces ______________________________

water condition ______________________________

Observations/Comments

____

____

____

____

____

____

____

____

INDEX

C

D

E

F

G

H

I

L

M

N

O

P

Q

R

S

T

V

W

Y